D0117596

BACKROAD WINERIES OF CALIFORNIA

A Discovery Tour of California's Country Wineries

Bill Gleeson

CHRONICLE BOOKS
San Francisco

Printed in the United States of America.

LIBRARY OF CONGRESS CATALOGING IN PUBLICATION DATA

Gleeson, Bill.
  Backroad wineries of California: a discovery tour of California's
country wineries / Bill Gleeson.
    p.   cm.

  Includes index.
  ISBN 0-87701-575-9
  1. Wine and wine making—California.   I. Title.
TP557.G57 1989   88-29267
641.2′2′025794—dc19   CIP

Editing: Carey Charlesworth
Cover illustration: Beth Whybrow Leeds

10 9 8 7 6 5 4 3 2 1

Chronicle Books
275 Fifth Street
San Francisco, California
94103

CONTENTS

Introduction

One skill that most every Californian masters early in life is waiting in line. We're the hands-down champs. We'll stand in a queue for two hours to ride Disneyland's "Star Tours," bear interminable stop-and-go freeway traffic to get to and from work, and wait half a day to buy a ticket for a 49ers game (and then wait in another long line to get into the stadium restroom).

So it should come as no great surprise that we're willing to endure the same congestion for the privilege of enjoying a "quiet, romantic getaway" to California's wine country.

Just take a look at the numbers of tourists who visit Napa Valley. On a busy day you'll join upwards of 15,000 other motorists on Highway 29 between Napa and Calistoga. The Mondavi Winery, alone, hosts more than a quarter-million visitors each year. It's as if we've come to accept wading through crowds as part of the California lifestyle.

While I can play the waiting game as well as the next guy, I'd rather not spend my valuable weekends stuck in Napa Valley traffic or (literally) rubbing elbows with a hundred others along a crowded tasting room bar. So I developed some alternative routes.

Instead of competing with the tourist traffic along the main highways, I began to explore the back roads. For example, rather than follow Highway 29 through Napa Valley, I much prefer snaking along Mt. Veeder road in the hills overlooking the congestion below. Enchanting Mayacamas Winery has a narrow, bumpy driveway no tour bus driver would dare attempt, and nearby Vose Vineyards offers visitors picnic areas with vistas unmatched in the region.

Similar alternatives exist in other winemaking regions of Northern and Southern California. Those venturing up to the scenic Uvas Valley out of Gilroy or Watsonville will meet winemaking folks like Terry and Mary Kaye Parks (Sycamore Creek Vineyards), who not only make the wine but pour it for visiting tasters. Farther south, the once remote Temecula Valley, now home to about a dozen small-to-large wineries, still exudes the folksy, rural charm that Napa Valley has all but lost.

If your wine country travels have been confined to the major highways, chances are you're quite familiar with names like Mondavi, Beringer, Almaden, and Krug. However, I'll wager you've not heard of Baily, Sarah's, Maurice Carrie, Nichelini, Nonini, or others that appear in the following pages.

This isn't to say that trips to the major wine-producing establishments are a waste of time. On the contrary, their modern equipment and techniques are impressive examples of advances in winemaking technology and are worth a look-see, especially for first-time winery visitors. But there is another, overlooked wine world in California. You'll be hard pressed to match a visit with—or tour or tasting led by—an owner, frequently an owner/vintner, who at many backroad wineries is responsible for tending the vines, operating the crusher, and polishing the bottles, too. Needless to say, each winery's "Vintner's Choice" or "Choices" arises from intimate knowledge of the offerings so specified in this book. (Where the vintner has declined to nominate a wine, I've offered my own choice.)

What distinguishes *Backroad Wineries of California* from other wine tour guides is that the owners of most of the wineries featured here do play personal, if not exclusive, roles in the production of their wares; all extend a friendly welcome to visitors—though some request a phone call in advance; and each is pleasantly situated off the beaten path.

By the way, don't let a "by appointment" note discourage you. While many do interpret such a statement as a discouragement, I found this not at all to be the intention of the owners. Because many small wineries are mom-and-pop-type operations, guests who drop in without advance word might find the proprietors out in the vineyard, working in the cellar, or otherwise earning their living. For most vintners, a phone call the day before your visit is more-than-sufficient notice. The call will be appreciated by the winemaker. And believe me, the visits you'll have will be well worth your extra effort.

THE SONOMA AND MENDOCINO COUNTY REGION

This Is Where It All Began

In the categories of natural beauty, history, and diversity of wineries, the Sonoma and Mendocino county areas are unsurpassed. From the lush redwood forests of the Russian River Valley to the rolling hills east of Ukiah, the scenery is nothing short of spectacular. Recreational opportunities abound, here.

The area's history is intricately tied to the grape. Agoston Haraszthy was the first to tap the commercial grape-growing potential of the Sonoma Valley—and of California, for that matter. Known as the father of California winemaking, Haraszthy established Buena Vista Winery—one of the state's first—and cultivated what once was the largest vineyard in the world. Your backroad tour of the Sonoma and Mendocino wine country begins, appropriately enough, at Haraszthy's old cellars.

Those who have followed the pioneer over the years have brought with them unique touches that set this region apart from all others. Even within an appellation (and there are many here), the individuality of different winemakers shines for all to enjoy. In the warm Alexander Valley near Healdsburg, for example, Alexander Valley Vineyards is headquartered in a contemporary, Spanish-style structure consisting of an adobe cellar topped with a veranda-shaded, board and batten tasting room. Just down the road Field Stone Winery sits below a grassy knoll, a natural stone facade providing the only clue to its subterranean existence.

Several other distinctive wineries call this region home. Hop Kiln Winery is housed in an historically significant hop kiln, while Hacienda Wine Cellars utilizes an old hospital. Farther north, near Ukiah, the owners of McDowell Valley Vineyards constructed a modern solar facility to showcase their wares.

Some forty wineries between Santa Rosa and Cloverdale are listed in a guide published by the Russian River Wine Road. For details, consult the Wine Tour Maps section at the back of this book. If your visit will include an overnight stay, you'll be interested in the guide's listing of resorts, motels, and bed and breakfast inns in the Russian River area, as well as in the recommendation and guide to additional inns below.

Spending the Night?

In Healdsburg, Madrona Manor, a beautifully restored inn and national historic landmark. 1001 Westside Road, Healdsburg, CA 95448; (707) 433-4231.

For a free copy of *Wine Country Inns of Sonoma County*, write to P.O. Box 51, Geyserville, CA 95441.

SONOMA TO SANTA ROSA

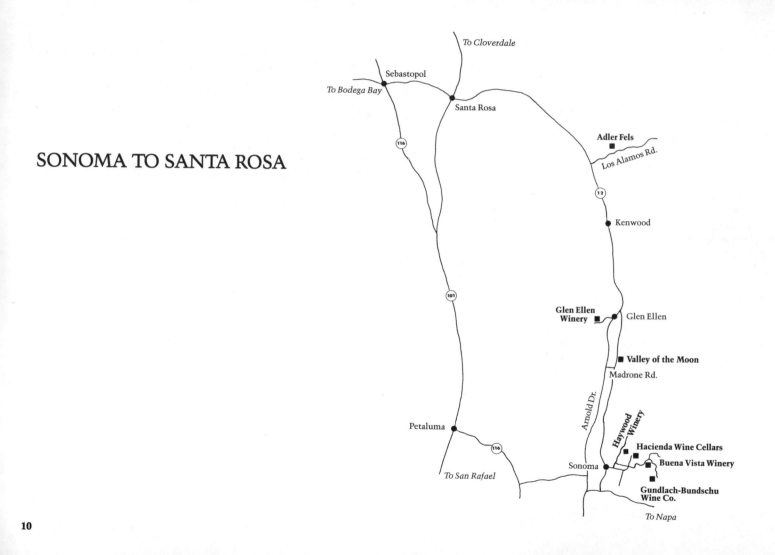

To Cloverdale

Sebastopol

To Bodega Bay

Santa Rosa

116

Adler Fels

Los Alamos Rd.

12

Kenwood

101

Glen Ellen Winery • Glen Ellen

■ **Valley of the Moon**

Madrone Rd.

Arnold Dr.

Haywood Winery

Petaluma

116

Hacienda Wine Cellars

Buena Vista Winery

To San Rafael

Sonoma

Gundlach-Bundschu Wine Co.

To Napa

Buena Vista Winery and Vineyards

Sonoma

For those with even the slightest interest in California wine, a visit to Buena Vista Winery on the outskirts of Sonoma is a must. It was here that the state's wine industry began, more than 130 years ago.

If Buena Vista is the birthplace of California wines (some historians disagree), Agoston Haraszthy, the Hungarian aristocrat turned California vintner, must be the patriarch of the industry.

A one-time bodyguard of Emperor Ferdinand of Austria-Hungary, Haraszthy fled his homeland after being marked for death following a revolution in the 1840s. He landed in the United States and travelled from east to west scouting a vineyard site. Haraszthy's twelve-year search ended in the Sonoma Valley, where he built a winery in 1857.

Tunnels were carved into a hill of solid limestone; rock debris was shaped into blocks for construction of the exterior walls. (While the sturdy winery has survived for more than a century, the wine pioneer's palatial home was destroyed by a fire before 1900.)

In 1861 Haraszthy convinced the governor of California to send him to Europe to collect *vinifera* vines. "The Count" returned with some 100,000 cuttings, which were distributed to growers throughout the region. In the years immediately following Haraszthy's death, in 1869, the vineyard at Buena Vista was the largest in the world, boasting nearly a half-million cuttings.

Haraszthy's wine empire wasn't spared, however, from a devastating phylloxera plague, nor from the 1906 earthquake, during which the Buena Vista tunnels collapsed. The operation bounced back in 1943 when the vineyards were replanted and buildings restored.

Tastings take place today in the original press house, a fine stone building with tile floors and an art gallery on the second level. Visitors may guide

18000 Old Winery Road
Sonoma, CA 95476
(707) 938-1266

HOURS: 10 A.M.–5 P.M. daily
TASTINGS: Yes
TOURS: Yes, self-guided
PICNIC AREA: Yes
RETAIL SALES: Yes
DIRECTIONS: From downtown Sonoma, east on East Napa Street, left on Old Winery Road to winery gate.
VINTNER'S CHOICE: Cabernet Sauvignon

themselves through the old cellar, where historical information and photos tell the Haraszthy story. This facility serves as headquarters for the Knights of the Vine, the nation's only wine brotherhood.

Unbeknownst to most who visit the historic Sonoma winery, there is another large, state-of-the-art facility operated by Buena Vista in the Carneros region. This newer winery is equipped to crush 150 tons of grapes per day and has a storage capacity of nearly one million gallons.

Fortunately, the corporation that owns Buena Vista has imposed no such modern trappings on Haraszthy's old stomping grounds in Sonoma. In fact, vehicular traffic here has wisely been restricted from the winery area, which further enhances the vintage ambience at this California wine shrine.

Hacienda Wine Cellars

Sonoma

Hacienda Wine Cellar shares with its neighbor, Buena Vista Winery, the historic vineyard cultivated by California wine pioneer Agoston Haraszthy in the mid-nineteenth century.

The vast plantings, which at one time had no equal in the world, were rescued from years of neglect in 1941 by Frank Bartholomew, former head of United Press International. Over the next several years, Bartholomew pumped new life into Haraszthy's historic Buena Vista Winery and replanted the vineyards. He sold Buena Vista some time later, retaining only fifty acres of vines.

His absence from the winemaking scene was short-lived, however. The lure of the grape brought Bartholomew back into the business in 1973 when he transformed the old Sonoma Valley Hospital into Hacienda Wine Cellars.

The 1920s-era Mediterranean-style building, whose original purpose was the care of patients, turned out to be equally well suited to the care of wine. Fourteen-inch-thick brick walls help maintain a fairly consistent temperature for the aging vintages. The production area is sealed off from the tasting room by a glass door, through which visitors can catch a glimpse of fancy chandeliers that illuminate rows of neatly stacked barrels along a tiled floor.

Outside, a row of ornamental vines shares the front yard with a number of plants and trees. The well-manicured gardens here are a favorite of picknickers, who congregate at tables under spreading oak trees.

1000 Vineyard Lane
Sonoma, CA 95476
(707) 938-3220

HOURS: 10 A.M.–5 P.M. daily
TASTINGS: Yes
TOURS: By appointment
PICNIC AREA: Yes
RETAIL SALES: Yes
DIRECTIONS: From downtown Sonoma, east on East Napa Street, left on East Seventh Street; follow signs to Vineyard Lane.
VINTNER'S CHOICE: Chardonnay and Chenin Blanc

Haywood Winery

Sonoma

A political science degree from Stanford, the Marines, a career in the construction industry . . . hardly the stuff of a successful winemaker, you say? It didn't seem to deter Peter Haywood, who parlayed a home winemaking hobby into a full-fledged winery that turns out some 20,000 cases per year.

Established in 1980, Haywood Winery is one of Sonoma's newest. The facility, which blends well with the surrounding volcanic cliffs and native oak, was built into a hillside, crafted from local field stone and concrete, and covered with sod.

Inside, the small stainless steel tanks total a 50,000-gallon capacity. The wine list here includes Chardonnay, White Riesling, Fumé Blanc, Cabernet Sauvignon, and Zinfandel.

Haywood has made considerable progress since his home winemaking days. He recalls—with both fondness and horror—his first attempt, in 1977, when 19 of the 20 bottles produced exploded. The remaining bottle, treasured like a businessman's first dollar bill, today rests in the Haywood library.

18701 Gehricke Road
Sonoma, CA 95476
(707) 996-4298

HOURS: 11 A.M.–5 P.M. daily
TASTINGS: Yes
TOURS: Yes
PICNIC AREA: Yes
RETAIL SALES: Yes
DIRECTIONS: In Sonoma, east on Napa Street, left on Fourth Street East, right on Lovall Valley Road, and left on Gehricke to winery.
AUTHOR'S CHOICE: Chardonnay

1986
ESTATE BOTTLED
WHITE RIESLING
SONOMA VALLEY
HAYWOOD
Residual sugar 1.6% by wt. Alcohol 11.2% by vol.
Grown, produced and bottled at 18701 Gehricke Rd.
HAYWOOD WINERY, SONOMA, CALIFORNIA

Gundlach-Bundschu Wine Company
Vineburg

Jacob Gundlach's persistent struggle to start a new life as a California winemaker was marked both by hardship and good fortune. First there was the storm that wrecked his ship on the trip around Cape Horn from Europe. He spent forty-nine days as an island castaway before reaching San Francisco in 1851.

Next came the backbreaking cultivation of his 400-acre Rhinefarm in Sonoma Valley with a horse-drawn single-blade plow, and the arduous process of hand-picking grapes and hauling sixty-pound lugs.

In 1874 the destructive insect called phylloxera worked its way through California's vineyards and into Gundlach's prized vines. Fortunately, Rhinefarm vineyard master Julius Dresel discovered that native American vines resisted the disease, and work began to graft the domestic rootstock onto the existing vines.

Things improved over the next few years as Jacob and his partner, son-in-law Charles Bundschu, built a thriving business, winning a loyal following and prestigious awards for their wines.

Tragedy struck again in 1906, when Jacob watched the great earthquake and fire turn his San Francisco cellars into ashes. Rhinefarm was untouched, however, and the business continued.

The next disastrous blow was dealt not by nature but by the government. Although the vineyards were cultivated during Prohibition, the winery closed its doors, and Gundlach-Bundschu was disbanded. A fire later gutted the abandoned winery.

Walter Bundschu, Jacob's great-grandson, took over the operation and was succeeded by his son, Towle Bundschu. Towle's son Jim revitalized the company by rebuilding the winery in the early 1970s using stone from the original building. The production area occupies most of the building. The tasting area is inside the front door, over which hangs an old bell from the original vineyards. Jacob Gundlach would have been proud.

2000 Denmark Street
Vineburg, CA 95487
(707) 938-5277

HOURS: 11 A.M.–4:30 P.M. daily
TASTINGS: Yes
TOURS: No
PICNIC AREA: Yes
RETAIL SALES: Yes
DIRECTIONS: From Sonoma, east on Napa Street, right on Eighth Street East, left on Denmark Street.
VINTNER'S CHOICE: Merlot

EST. 1858

GUNDLACH
BUNDSCHU

Estate Bottled

1987
DRESEL'S
SONOMA VALLEY
SONOMA RIESLING
PRODUCED AND BOTTLED BY
GUNDLACH BUNDSCHU WINERY B.W. 64
VINEBURG, CALIFORNIA 95487
ALCOHOL 12.7% BY VOLUME

Glen Ellen Winery

Glen Ellen

Upon discovering a derelict vineyard in 1979 on writer Jack London's old stomping grounds, Mike Benziger placed an excited call to his parents' home in White Plains, New York. "Dad, I've found it!" he told Bruno Benziger, signaling the beginning of a new life for the family and the birth of Glen Ellen Winery.

Several years earlier, Mike had moved to California to learn the art of winemaking and to find a spot where his family could make wine together. After Mike's discovery, brothers Joe, Bobby, and Jerry and their families; younger brother Chris; sister Kathy; Bruno and Helen Benziger; and Bruno's mother, Katherine—thirteen in all—packed up and left their native New York, settling into two old homes on the property in the hills above Glen Ellen.

The neglected vineyards had seen many a harvest since the late 1860s, when Julius Wegener was given 122 acres by Mexican Gov. Mariano Vallejo. In addition to a winemaking operation, Wegener's ranch served as a popular resort. The two residences built by Wegener today house the Benziger clan. A building that doubled in the old days as a church and dance hall stood where the swimming pool is now.

Although Wegener's family lived on the ranch for many years after his death, the vineyards declined. Nevertheless, some wine was marketed: An old Wegener diary contains references to purchases by Jack London, whose ranch was next door.

In restoring the tired estate, the Benzigers revived the two houses using period materials and furnishings. Most of the vines were replanted. A classic wooden barn is used for winemaking. A tasting area shares the building with barrels and fermenting tanks.

Visitors who have questions about the making of Glen Ellen wines need only ask the nearest person. Odds are he or she will be a Benziger.

1883 London Ranch Road
Glen Ellen, CA 95442
(707) 996-1066

HOURS: 10 A.M.–4 P.M. daily
TASTINGS: Yes
TOURS: Yes
PICNIC AREA: Yes
RETAIL SALES: Yes
DIRECTIONS: From Arnold Road in Glen Ellen, 1 mile up London Ranch Road to winery gate.
VINTNER'S CHOICE: Sauvignon Blanc

Adler Fels

Santa Rosa

Of the wineries I have visited, none appears so much a product of a single individual as Adler Fels. This is, quite literally, the winery that David Coleman built.

A graphic designer by original trade, David was introduced to the wine industry in 1974 while conceiving the label design for Chateau St. Jean. One assignment led to another, and before long David had earned a reputation as one of California's premier wine label designers. In the process he also learned a great deal about the art of winemaking.

David's decision to start a winery was hatched in 1979 during an evening of intemperate wine tasting with friend and original partner Pat Heck. Ground was broken in 1979 on a tree-studded hilltop overlooking much of Sonoma Valley. David constructed the winery by hand, adding a tower and cupola that give the building a fairytale appearance from the approaching drive.

The interior, absent any such flourishes, is intended for serious winemaking. Here stands a row of special fermentors designed by the owner. It was David who perfected the variable-capacity fermentation tank whose free-floating top adjusts to the level of wine inside. Such tanks are now in use throughout the state.

David's influence doesn't stop here, for after the aging process, the wines are bottled under a label designed by—guess who?

Adler Fels (German for "Eagle Rock," the name of a landmark outcropping visible from the winery tower) does rely also on the talents of others, including Ayn Ryan. Ayn (pronounced Ann) joined the business in 1980 to direct sales efforts and shortly thereafter married David. Reminiscing about the frantic pace of Adler Fels' initial year, Ayn recalled that, "After surviving our first crush, we figured together we could make anything work." And they have.

5325 Corrick Lane
Santa Rosa, CA 95405
(707) 539-3123

HOURS: By appointment
TASTINGS: By appointment
TOURS: By appointment
PICNIC AREA: No
RETAIL SALES: Yes, by appointment
DIRECTIONS: From Highway 12, 2 miles north on Los Alamos Road to Corrick Lane and winery gate.
VINTNER'S CHOICE: Fumé Blanc

Valley of the Moon Winery

Glen Ellen

Harry Parducci has spent much of his life at Valley of the Moon Winery. His father, Enrico, bought the business in 1941, acquiring an assortment of buildings along with vineyards that dated back to 1851.

The younger Parducci worked with his father for a number of years before assuming the helm in 1971. Harry's sons have more recently joined the family business.

Valley of the Moon produces some 48,000 cases each year from its facilities near Sonoma Creek. Wine buffs are unfortunately limited to the harvest period for a view of the inner workings. During most of the year, visits are confined to a small tasting room at the front of the winery, under the spreading branches of a formidable bay laurel.

Valley of the Moon rounds out its roster of estate-bottled, 100 percent varietal and table wines with a selection of dessert wines, as well as champagne.

777 Madrone Road
Glen Ellen, CA 95442
(707) 996-6941

HOURS: 10 A.M.–6 P.M. Every day
TASTINGS: Yes
TOURS: During harvest
PICNIC AREA: Yes
RETAIL SALES: Yes
DIRECTIONS: .4 miles west of Highway 12 on Madrone Road near Arnold Drive.
VINTNER'S CHOICE: Black Label Reserve Zinfandel

FORESTVILLE TO CLOVERDALE

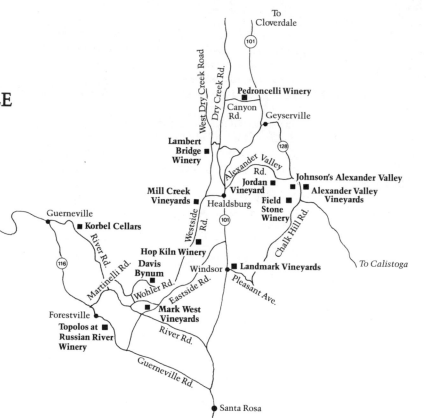

To Cloverdale

101

Pedroncelli Winery ■

West Dry Creek Road

Dry Creek Rd.

Canyon Rd.

Geyserville ●

Lambert Bridge Winery ■

128

Alexander Valley Rd.

Johnson's Alexander Valley ■

Jordan Vineyard ■

Alexander Valley Vineyards ■

Mill Creek Vineyards ■

Healdsburg

Field Stone Winery ■

Westside Rd.

101

Chalk Hill Rd.

Guerneville ●

Korbel Cellars ■

To Calistoga

River Rd.

Hop Kiln Winery ■

Davis Bynum ■

116

Windsor ●

Landmark Vineyards ■

Martinelli Rd.

Wohler Rd.

Eastside Rd.

Pleasant Ave.

Forestville ●

Mark West Vineyards ■

Topolos at Russian River Winery ■

River Rd.

Guerneville Rd.

Santa Rosa ●

Topolos at Russian River

Topolos at Russian River Vineyards

Forestville

Question: What do you get by crossing the architectue of a hop kiln with that of Fort Ross? Answer: A decidely unique winery.

The concrete and redwood building that now houses Topolos at Russian River Winery is a peculiar hybrid. Its builders combined striking elements of the region's old hop kilns with nineteenth-century Russian architecture found at the coastal settlement of Fort Ross. The weathered building has undoubtedly sparked the curiosity of many who travel the Gravenstein Highway between Guerneville and Sebastopol.

The winery was founded in 1978 by vintner Michael Topolos and his brother, Jerry, a Bay Area businessman. Michael was motivated by years of touring European wineries as a merchant *du vin* for a San Francisco grocer and by studies at the University of California, Davis. He is also an author of California wine books and has taught wine appreciation courses at area colleges.

The unusual-looking winery is only part of the Russian River Vineyards complex. The establishment is one of few in California with a full restaurant. The quaint dining room is housed on the upper level of an adjacent century-old residence. The bottom portion serves as a tasting room and gift shop. Among the wines available here are Zinfandel, Petite Sirah, and Alicante Bouschet.

5700 Gravenstein Highway
Forestville, CA 95436
(707) 887-2956

HOURS: 10:30 A.M.–5 P.M. Wednesday–Sunday
TASTINGS: Yes
TOURS: By appointment
PICNIC AREA: No
RETAIL SALES: Yes
DIRECTIONS: In Forestville on Highway 116 (the Gravenstein Highway).
VINTNER'S CHOICE: Petite Sirah

TOPOLOS
at Russian River Vineyards

Sonoma Mountain

Sonoma County

Zinfandel
Ultimo
1983

PRODUCED & BOTTLED BY **TOPOLOS**
AT RUSSIAN RIVER VINEYARDS, FORESTVILLE, CA
ALCOHOL 12.9% BY VOLUME

Mark West Vineyards

Forestville

With the thousands of vehicles that daily zoom along River Road between Highway 101 and Guerneville, it's amazing that more of them don't find their way to little Mark West Vineyards, which sits quietly only a stone's throw from the bustling thoroughfare.

I found Mark West to be a friendly, relaxing, informal place to linger for awhile. On my visit I poked about the well-stocked tasting room and gift shop, roamed the winery grounds, and relaxed at a picnic table under shady trees.

Bob and Joan Ellis (viticulturist and winemaker, respectively) run the show here. Mark West is actually the name of a little creek that runs along the property. The Ellises produce about 22,000 cases per year of Chardonnay, Gewürz-traminer, Pinot Noir, Zinfandel, Johannisberg Riesling, Pinot Noir Blanc, late-harvest wines, and sparkling wine.

The Ellises prefer to handcraft their wines, and likewise devote personal attention to the affairs of the winery. Don't be surprised if the person behind the tasting room bar is one of the owners.

7000 Trenton-Healdsburg Road
Forestville, CA 95436
(707) 544-4813

HOURS: 10 A.M.–5 P.M. daily
TASTINGS: Yes
TOURS: Yes
PICNIC AREA: Yes
RETAIL SALES: Yes
DIRECTIONS: West off Highway 101 on River Road, 5.5 miles to Trenton-Healdsburg Road, right for .5 mile to winery (on left).
AUTHOR'S CHOICE: Pinot Noir Blanc

Lambert Bridge Winery

Healdsburg

Just as the wineries that hug Napa Valley's Route 29 attract that area's largest number of tourists, the wine operations situated along Highway 101 in Sonoma County are the most successful at luring the lion's share of this region's visitors. All the more reason to pull off and explore some of the Sonoma County area's less-travelled byways. And there are many from which to choose.

One of my new-found favorite locales is the Dry Creek Valley. Not only is the scenery appealing, some local association has marked the valley's "major" intersections with helpful directional signs pointing the way to dozens of small wineries with unfamiliar names. On my latest Dry Creek sojourn, I followed the arrows across Lambert Bridge to its namesake winery.

A longtime resident of Southern California, Gerard Lambert left a career in real estate to move north in 1968. He and his wife, Babbie, built their rustic, barn-inspired winery in 1975, a half-dozen years after buying 100 or so acres of fertile valley land. The first vineyards of Cabernet were planted here in 1970, followed by plantings of Pinot Noir, Chardonnay, Merlot, and Johannisberg Riesling. Lambert Bridge became one of the region's first small wineries to produce strictly estate-bottled wines in three varieties: Cabernet, Chardonnay, and Merlot.

A small, family-managed operation (owned by the Seagram Wine Company), Lambert Bridge is not set up to offer tastings. However, tours of the picturesque winery are available (by appointment), and visitors may purchase a bottle of wine and linger at a picnic table along the lane.

4085 West Dry Creek Road
Healdsburg, CA 95448
(707) 433-5855

HOURS: Monday–Friday, by appointment
TASTINGS: No
TOURS: By appointment
PICNIC AREA: By appointment
RETAIL SALES: By appointment
DIRECTIONS: From Highway 101 north of Healdsburg, west on Lytton Springs Road, right on Dry Creek Road, left on Lambert Bridge Road, and left on West Dry Creek Road to winery.
VINTNER'S CHOICE: Chardonnay

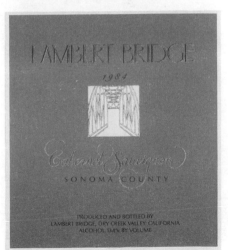

Mill Creek Vineyards

Healdsburg

No, you're not in New England. It is definitely Sonoma County. Inside this old mill is a wine tasting room.

This unique wine country creation was made possible through the efforts of two generations of the Kreck family. Chuck (Dad) is the proprietor; Vera (Mom) manages the tasting room; sons William and Robert work as general manager and winemaster, respectively.

While the wine list is a comprehensive one (the Krecks produce Chardonnay, Sauvignon Blanc, Gewürztraminer, Cabernet Blush, Gamay Beaujolais, Pinot Noir, Merlot, and Cabernet Sauvignon), chances are the vintages won't be what draws you to this establishment. This is one of the most picturesque wineries in these parts, and a favorite among passing shutterbugs intrigued by the mill and its working water wheel.

A lesser known but equally impressive attraction is Mill Creek's wonderful picnic deck, situated at the top of the hill behind the winery. When you visit Mill Creek, plan to drop by around lunchtime, sandwiches in hand.

1401 Westside Road
Healdsburg, CA 95448
(707) 433-5098

HOURS: 10 A.M.–4:30 P.M. daily in summer; noon–5 P.M. Thursday and Friday only, the rest of the year
TASTINGS: Yes
TOURS: Yes
PICNIC AREA: Yes
RETAIL SALES: Yes
DIRECTIONS: From Highway 101, north at Healdsburg exit, left at first stop sign (Westside Road) to winery.
AUTHOR'S CHOICE: Gewürztraminer

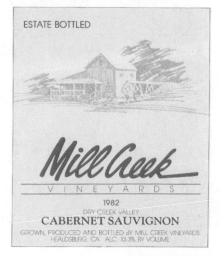

ESTATE BOTTLED

Mill Creek
VINEYARDS
1982
DRY CREEK VALLEY
CABERNET SAUVIGNON
GROWN, PRODUCED AND BOTTLED BY MILL CREEK VINEYARDS
HEALDSBURG, CA ALC. 13.5% BY VOLUME

Hop Kiln Winery
Healdsburg

Question Martin Griffin about his seemingly peculiar combination of careers in public health and winemaking and he'll remind you of Louis Pasteur, noted bacteriologist and chief winemaker for France. The Griffin name isn't likely to go down in history with that of Pasteur, but Martin's contributions to both fields have earned him great respect throughout Northern California.

His first career included nearly twenty years as a doctor of internal medicine at a Marin County clinic he helped establish. Martin later switched careers for a brief time, performing wildlife work in such locales as Hawaii and India. He subsequently earned a master's degree in public health and became a public health officer at Sonoma State Hospital.

While he had since the 1960s held the ingredients for a winemaking operation (a 240-acre Healdsburg ranch with several acres of vines), it wasn't until the 1970s that Martin turned serious attention to establishing a winery.

The logical site was a turn-of-the-century hop kiln and cooling and baling barn, which he and friends painstakingly restored from a crumbling hulk. Martin chose as his residence a stately Italianate Victorian, which was moved in pieces from Fulton and reassembled next to the kiln. The establishment opened as Hop Kiln Winery in 1975.

Visitors are received in the spacious barn-turned-tasting-room behind the tall kilns. A row of picture windows along the back wall illuminates the rustic interior and reveals a sweeping vista of vineyards and adjacent pond. Picnic tables are set up along the edge of the water.

While Hop Kiln has won numerous wine awards, Martin is most proud of the preservation efforts that pumped new life into the old barn and kiln. His pride is shared by the federal government, which has confirmed the winery's place in the future by declaring Hop Kiln a National Trust.

6050 Westside Road
Healdsburg, CA 95448
(707) 433-6491

HOURS: 10 A.M.–5 P.M. daily
TASTINGS: Yes
TOURS: By appointment
PICNIC AREA: Yes
RETAIL SALES: Yes
DIRECTIONS: From Mill Street in Healdsburg, south on Westside Road to winery.
VINTNER'S CHOICE: Zinfandel

1985
A THOUSAND FLOWERS
Sonoma County Dry Table Wine
Alcohol 12.5% by Volume
Contains Sulfites
Produced and Bottled by the Hop Kiln Winery at Griffin Vineyard, Healdsburg, Sonoma County, California

Davis Bynum Winery
Healdsburg

Hop Kiln Winery isn't the only Russian River Valley winemaking operation set up in a hop-drying facility. You might not recognize the similarities, but the nondescript building that houses Davis Bynum Winery also did time as the area's most modern hop kiln.

The area surrounding the winery was found to be well suited to growing not only hops but Chardonnay, Sauvignon Blanc, Gewürztraminer, and Pinot Noir grapes, all of which are represented in the Davis Bynum wine line. Bynum Cabernet Sauvignon comes from nearby Dry Creek and Alexander Valley.

Like many backroad winemakers, Davis Bynum didn't fancy himself a vintner when planning his career. Rather, his initial training was in journalism. Winemaking surfaced later as a hobby during a stint as a reporter for a San Francisco newspaper. It wasn't until after more than a dozen years as a home winemaker that Bynum took the plunge, establishing his original winery in Albany.

Although production is climbing to upwards of 35,000 cases annually, the operation is still small enough to retain its family orientation. Bynum's son, Hampton, formerly the winemaker, now coordinates national sales efforts, and his wife, Dorothy, heads the "landscaping-building-improvement program." In addition, Dorothy's art has been featured on past "artist lables" for Bynum wines.

8075 Westside Road
Healdsburg, CA 95448
(707) 433-5852

HOURS: 10 A.M.–5 P.M. daily
TASTINGS: Yes
TOURS: By appointment
PICNIC AREA: Yes
RETAIL SALES: Yes
DIRECTIONS: From Highway 101 at Healdsburg, west (then south) on Westside Road for 8 miles.
VINTNER'S CHOICES: Cabernet Sauvignon and Chardonnay

RESERVE BOTTLING
DAVIS BYNUM
1987
Russian River Valley
GEWURZTRAMINER
McIlroy Vineyard
Produced & Bottled By Davis Bynum Winery
HEALDSBURG, SONOMA COUNTY, CA. ALC. 11.9% BY VOL. CONTAINS SULFITES

Korbel Champagne Cellars

Guerneville

Visitors are invited to step into Champagne-making history at Korbel. Framed by stately redwoods, this venerable, ivy-covered winery has been producing Champagne since the Korbel brothers set up shop here in the 1880s. On display for tour groups are antiques and vintage photos that are as interesting as the production process. Tours are also offered of the lushly restored Korbel compound gardens.

The Korbels, who owned the winery for more than a half century, sold the operation to the Heck family in 1954. Gary Heck, who started his career as the winery's assistant office manager, today serves as its president and CEO.

The Korbel Cellars produce more than one million cases per year of Champagne, made according to the *méthode champenoise*, in which the product is fermented not in a tank but inside the bottle. The process involves blending wines into a *cuvée* and bottling them with a special yeast and a bit of sugar.

The Korbel line includes a half dozen or so Champagnes. The Rosé is made from Pinot Noir grapes, and a Blanc de Blanc is crafted from Chardonnay grapes. Still made here is Korbel Sec, the cellars' very first release of a hundred years ago.

The directions below offer the most straightforward route, from Highway 101. But if your winery itinerary permits, one of your best bets is a trip into the Russian River Valley out Westside Road from Healdsburg. This back road will guide you past other picturesque wineries as well, such as Hop Kiln and Mill Creek.

13250 River Road
Guerneville, CA 95446
(707) 887-2294

HOURS: 9 A.M.–5 P.M. daily
TASTINGS: Yes
TOURS: Yes
PICNIC AREA: Yes
RETAIL SALES: Yes
DIRECTIONS: From Highway 101, 3 miles north of Santa Rosa, west on River Road for 12 miles to winery (or follow directions from Healdsburg in text).
VINTNER'S CHOICE: Korbel Natural

Landmark Vineyards

Windsor

Notwithstanding the creep of development around the Sonoma County town of Windsor, Landmark Vineyards has managed to maintain its bucolic setting amid century-old stands of trees and acres of vineland.

A winery only since 1974, the "home ranch," as the owners refer to it, originally was a portion of a land grant that was settled in 1849 by the McClellan family. A stately Spanish-style residence was built several years later by a McClellan heir and later was home to the shipping magnate William Matson-Roth. The house now holds the tasting room and offices of Landmark Vineyards, established by William Mabry, Jr.; his wife, Maxine; and son, William III. Young Bill is winemaker and president of Landmark.

The purchase of the Windsor estate was the Mabrys' final step toward establishing their winemaking operation. The family had in the preceding two years bought grape-growing land in Sonoma and Alexander valleys.

On the historic home ranch the Mabrys built a modern winery that draws its design inspiration from the adjacent main house. Landmark has limited its production to just one wine—Chardonnay—as well as a second line of vintages labeled "Cypress Lane Vineyards."

Visitors enter the property via an avenue flanked by towering cypress trees planted by the ranch founders. Equally impressive are the gardens, also dating from long ago. A wooded creekside area, open to Landmark guests, holds picnic tables and an outdoor fireplace and barbecue. The production facilities may be toured by appointment.

9150 Los Amigos Road
Windsor, CA 95492
(707) 838-9708

HOURS: 10 A.M.–5 P.M. Friday–Sunday
TASTINGS: Yes
TOURS: By appointment
PICNIC AREA: Yes
RETAIL SALES: Yes
DIRECTIONS: From Highway 101, take Windsor exit, east to Lakewood, turn left; left at Brooks to winery drive (Los Amigos Road).
VINTNER'S CHOICE: Chardonnay

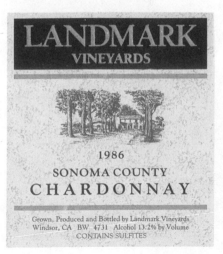

Field Stone Winery

Healdsburg

Unlike most conventional wineries, built from the ground up, Field Stone was built from the ground down. The late Wallace Johnson chose a natural oak-studded knoll on his ranch and in the mid 1970s proceeded to carve out a long, narrow slice of earth.

After lining the walls with concrete and building a ceiling, workers redistributed soil over the bunker, returning the knoll to a reasonable facsimile of its former self. The field stone used to construct the facade was that unearthed during excavation. This intriguing underground facility is said to be the only known winery of its kind built in California since 1900.

Wallace, an inventor of portable aluminum scaffolding, purchased the property in 1955 to pursue an interest in raising purebred cattle. However, after soil tests a few years later showed the ranch to be well suited to grapevines, Redwood Hereford Ranch evolved into Redwood Ranch and Vineyard. Construction of Field Stone came on the heels of an auspicious planting effort that began in the mid sixties.

Unfortunately, the rancher-turned-vintner lived to see few crushes at Field Stone. Wallace died in 1979, and the winery passed to his daughter, Katrina, and son-in-law, Dr. John Staten.

Although Katrina had become familiar with the business while serving for many years as secretary-treasurer for her father, John was pursuing an unrelated career in theological education. Redirecting his efforts, he eagerly set out to earn his new titles of vintner and general manager. Field Stone has during the past few years also utilized the talents of consulting enologist André Tchelistcheff and winemaker James Thomson.

The efficient winery, bulging with modern tanks and equipment, is open for tours by appointment. Visitors will catch a glimpse of the production area on the way to the redwood-panelled tasting room, which is open daily. A number of tree-shaded picnic tables are scattered about the winery grounds.

10075 Highway 128
Healdsburg, CA 95448
(707) 433-7266

HOURS: 10 A.M.–5 P.M. daily; closed
Christmas and New Year's
TASTINGS: Yes
TOURS: By appointment
PICNIC AREA: Yes
RETAIL SALES: Yes
DIRECTIONS: Near intersection of Highway 128 and Chalk Hill Road.
VINTNER'S CHOICE: Cabernet Sauvignon

FIELD STONE
ESTATE 1982 BOTTLED
SPRING-CABERNET
ALEXANDER VALLEY
GROWN, PRODUCED AND BOTTLED BY
REDWOOD RANCH AND VINEYARD • HEALDSBURG, CA
RESIDUAL SUGAR 1.5% • ALCOHOL 12.2% BY VOLUME

Alexander Valley Vineyards
Healdsburg

Wine grapes represent only one of myriad crops that have flourished on the estate now known as Alexander Valley Vineyards. In the 1840s Cyrus Alexander directed the establishment of a vast agricultural tract that included fruit trees, vegetable gardens, wheat fields, hops, and cattle and sheep ranches.

Recruited by landowner Henry Fitch to open the virgin northern section of his 300,000-acre Sotoyome Grant, Alexander became the first European settler of the valley that now bears his name.

After outgrowing his modest adobe, in 1906 Alexander constructed an ornate Victorian. The homesite and several hundred acres remained in the Alexander family until 1963, when Los Angeles manufacturing company executive Harry Wetzel, Jr., and a friend purchased the old home along with some land and set about planting vineyards. By 1973, the estate had grown to 240 acres.

Wetzel's son, Harry (Hank) III, and daughter, Katie Wetzel-Murphy, run the business from an Early California–style winery situated on a hillside a stone's throw from the restored Alexander homestead. The dark-stained board and batten tasting room and offices sit atop the cellar, whose walls are fashioned from adobe.

Visitors may sample Alexander Valley's estate-bottled wines in the antique-furnished tasting room or soak up countryside views from the veranda.

8644 Highway 128
Healdsburg, CA 95448
(707) 433-7209

HOURS: 10 A.M.–5 P.M. daily; closed major holidays
TASTINGS: Yes
TOURS: By appointment
PICNIC AREA: Yes
RETAIL SALES: Yes
DIRECTIONS: From Highway 101, east on Dry Creek Road, left on Healdsburg Avenue, right on Alexander Valley Road (becomes Highway 128), to winery drive.
VINTNER'S CHOICE: Chardonnay

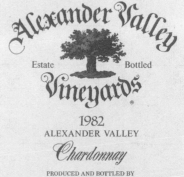

Estate — Bottled

Alexander Valley Vineyards

1982
ALEXANDER VALLEY
Chardonnay

PRODUCED AND BOTTLED BY
ALEXANDER VALLEY WINERY CO.
ALEXANDER VALLEY, HEALDSBURG, CALIFORNIA
ALCOHOL 13.6% BY VOLUME

Johnson's Alexander Valley Wines
Healdsburg

For this wine country traveler, meeting folks like Tom and Gail Johnson is what makes a visit to a small, family-owned winery a memorable experience. This happy clan isn't driven to set the wine world afire. For Tom, Gail, and their daughter and son, starting a small winery was a labor of love. But the business was a long time coming.

The land under Johnson's Alexander Valley Wines wasn't always oriented primarily to vineyards. The family farm began back in 1952 under the direction of Tom's father, as a fruit ranch, producing pears, plums, and some grapes.

A plot of premium vines was started in the mid 1960s, and a few years later Tom and Gail took over the ranch. The winery building, originally established in the 1880s, was refurbished, and the Johnsons' dream of opening a winery soon became a reality.

Tom heads the operation; Gail can often be found in the tasting room; and daughter Ellen, a Fresno State grad, fills the role of winemaker. A younger son occasionally pitches in behind the wheel of the family tractor.

Visitors to the Johnson property have been known to do double takes upon approaching the winery, where the sounds of a vintage theater pipe organ can occasionally be heard. The Johnsons crank up the contraption during harvest season, at the winery's annual anniversary party, for Tom's birthday, or when the mood (or the wine) inspires them.

8333 Highway 128
Healdsburg, CA 95448
(707) 433-2319

HOURS: 10 A.M.–5 P.M. daily (until 6 P.M. during summer months)
TASTINGS: Yes
TOURS: Given informally
PICNIC AREA: Yes
RETAIL SALES: Yes
DIRECTIONS: From Highway 101, east on Dry Creek Road, left on Healdsburg Avenue, right on Alexander Valley Road (becomes Highway 128) to winery. Johnson's is across the road to the north of Alexander Valley Vineyards (preceding).
VINTNER'S CHOICE: Pinot Noir

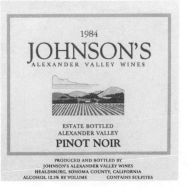

1984
JOHNSON'S
ALEXANDER VALLEY WINES

ESTATE BOTTLED
ALEXANDER VALLEY
PINOT NOIR

PRODUCED AND BOTTLED BY
JOHNSON'S ALEXANDER VALLEY WINES
HEALDSBURG, SONOMA COUNTY, CALIFORNIA
ALCOHOL 12.5% BY VOLUME   CONTAINS SULFITES

Jordan Vineyard and Winery

Healdsburg

If pressed to name one backcountry California winery as an absolute must-see, I immediately envision Tom Jordan's sprawling Bordeaux-style chateau in the Alexander Valley. Unfortunately, I can't tell you where it is, having sworn on a case of Cabernet not to divulge its exact location.

The good news is that the Jordan people will give you directions over the phone when you call for an appointment. (They're sticklers about appointments.)

The first hint of something special is the wide, highway-type drive that winds past moss-laden oaks from Alexander Valley Road. After twists and turns over a bridge or two, the mustard-colored winery unfolds in a magnificent scene right out of a French postcard. There is no other like it in California.

The baronial estate of Tom and Sally Jordan was established in the early 1970s, fulfilling the owners' longtime dream. Tom earned his fortune in oil exploration and sank a good chunk of it in these Sonoma County hills, striving to create wines that would compete with the best from France. In the process, he carved out hundreds of acres of new vineyards (Cabernet, Merlot, and Chardonnay) and erected what the *New York Times* called "one of the most spectacular wineries in North America."

Built at a cost estimated at between $15 and $20 million, the estate has been the site of countless lavish parties since its construction. In fact, the facilities are geared more to invited guests than drop-in visitors. The Jordans are entertainers par excellence, hosting elaborate feasts and wine celebrations primarily for those involved in marketing Jordan wines.

Visitors who take the public tour will catch some savory glimpses of the Jordan opulence. You'll be able to peek into the grand formal dining room and stroll through the pristine winemaking facilities, including a barrel room lit by chandeliers and framed by redwood beams. Unfortunately, you'll have to thumb through the winery brochure to see the exquisitely furnished guest suites upstairs.

In keeping with the Jordan tradition, you won't find a winery gift shop offering t-shirts and personalized corkscrews. There's not even a public tasting room. Wines are discreetly sold on site out of a large armoire.

P.O. Box 878
Healdsburg, CA 95448
(707) 433-6955

HOURS: By appointment
TASTINGS: No
TOURS: By appointment
PICNIC AREA: No
RETAIL SALES: By appointment
DIRECTIONS: Off Alexander Valley Road.
    Call winery for specific directions.
VINTNER'S CHOICE: Cabernet Sauvignon

Jordan

ESTATE BOTTLED
1984
Cabernet Sauvignon
Alexander Valley

GROWN, PRODUCED & BOTTLED BY JORDAN VINEYARD & WINERY
ALEXANDER VALLEY, HEALDSBURG, CALIF. ALCOHOL 12.5% BY VOLUME

J. Pedroncelli Winery

Geyserville

Second-generation winemakers John and Jim Pedroncelli learned the trade from their father, John Sr., who in 1927 bought the winery that bears the family name.

The elder Pedroncelli began by selling grapes, later making bulk wine. He cultivated the vines throughout Prohibition and sold field-mixed grapes to home winemakers. John began to bottle under his own name by the 1940s. His sons were introduced to the winemaker's way of life as youngsters, pulling weeds and plowing the vineyards. John Jr. was named winemaker in 1948, and a few years later Jim took over the business aspects of the winery. Ownership had passed to the siblings by 1963.

Pedroncelli's somewhat compact appearance is a bit deceptive, as some 125,000 gallons are produced here each year. Tasting takes place at a newer room in a barrel storage building overlooking a Zinfandel vineyard. Among the near-dozen varietals available at Pedroncelli is Zinfandel Rosé, a longtime popular wine made from 100 percent Zinfandel grapes.

1220 Canyon Road
Geyserville, CA 95441
(707) 857-3531

HOURS: 10 A.M.–5 P.M. daily; closed major holidays
TASTINGS: Yes
TOURS: By appointment
PICNIC AREA: No
RETAIL SALES: Yes
DIRECTIONS: One mile west of Highway 101 on Canyon Road.
VINTNER'S CHOICE: Zinfandel

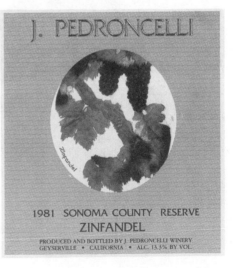

J. PEDRONCELLI

1981 SONOMA COUNTY RESERVE
ZINFANDEL

PRODUCED AND BOTTLED BY J. PEDRONCELLI WINERY
GEYSERVILLE • CALIFORNIA • ALC. 13.5% BY VOL.

HOPLAND TO REDWOOD VALLEY

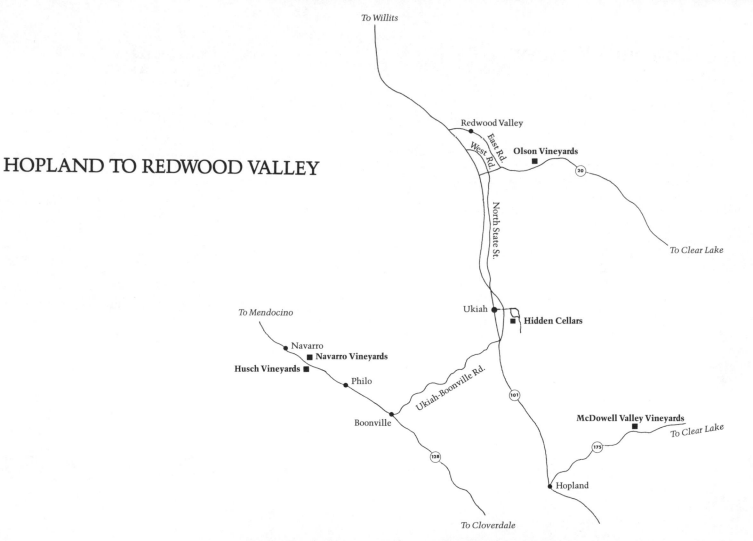

To Willits

Redwood Valley

East Rd.

West Rd.

Olson Vineyards ■

20

To Clear Lake

North State St.

Ukiah ●

■ **Hidden Cellars**

To Mendocino

Navarro ●

■ **Navarro Vineyards**

Husch Vineyards ■

Philo ●

Ukiah-Boonville Rd.

Boonville ●

101

McDowell Valley Vineyards ■

175

To Clear Lake

128

Hopland ●

To Cloverdale

McDowell Valley Vineyards
Hopland

Having learned in advance of my visit that McDowell Valley Vineyards held the distinction of being California's first solar winery, I visualized a makeshift building with a couple of unsightly solar panels stuck to the roof.

Contrary to my preconceptions, the facility revealed itself to be a handsome showplace of contemporary energy conservation and one of the most impressive small winemaking operations in the state, if not the nation. An imposing sight even from the highway some distance away, the winery is particularly awe inspiring up close. The sprawling building is an artful arrangement of berms, beams, solar cells, decks, and windows nestled amongst 360 acres of vines, some of which are more than a half century old.

McDowell Valley's recent designation as a distinct grape-growing appellation was the culmination of efforts by owners Karen and Richard Keehn, who documented the unique climatic and soil qualities here after establishing their winery in 1979.

The ground floor of the building, partially concealed behind a cooling earthen berm, holds a series of production, storage, fermentation, and bottling chambers. The second floor houses the tasting room, laboratory, catering kitchen, offices, and picnic decks. An expansive tasting room, which contains a baby grand piano for special events, is the centerpiece of the winery.

The facility's mechanical solar equipment includes 600 square feet of solar collectors, a complex water circulation system, and heat exchangers. The more subtle passive elements—such as double-paned windows, skylights, and berms—serve to enhance not only the energy self-sufficiency of the building but its sleek appearance as well.

A few years ago, McDowell joined the ranks of local wineries that have opened tasting rooms in Hopland. While many tasters will be content to sample McDowell wines in this convenient setting, it's well worth the extra few miles to see the source.

3811 Highway 175
Hopland, CA 95449
(707) 744-1053

HOURS: 10 A.M.–5 P.M. weekends
TASTINGS: Weekends only
TOURS: Weekends by appointment
PICNIC AREA: Yes
RETAIL SALES: Yes
DIRECTIONS: From Hopland, east on Highway 175, 4 miles to winery sign.
VINTNER'S CHOICE: Syrah

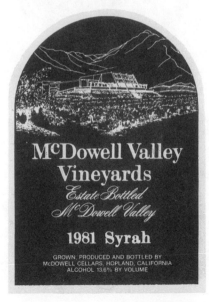

McDowell Valley Vineyards
Estate Bottled
McDowell Valley

1981 Syrah

GROWN, PRODUCED AND BOTTLED BY
McDOWELL CELLARS, HOPLAND, CALIFORNIA
ALCOHOL 13.6% BY VOLUME

Hidden Cellars

Ukiah

The odds weren't in the corner of Mendocino County farmer Dennis Patton when he set out to establish a winery in the early 1980s. He had only a converted garage in which to practice his craft, the United States was in recession, interest rates were inching past 20 percent, and the domestic wine market was being flooded by European imports.

Armed with pocket change that was bolstered by sweat equity and optimism, Patton persevered. Thousands of cases and dozens of award ribbons later, Hidden Cellars is now enjoying the life it deserves in newer digs on the Hildreth Ranch outside of Ukiah. Not that the winery has graduated to the big leagues. Production has leveled off at about 10,000 cases per year, and labels (an unusual spiral wrapper) are still applied by hand.

The Hidden Cellars tasting bar is situated in the winery warehouse, giving visitors the chance to see much of the operation up close and personal. Outside, a picnic area looks out over foothills and vineyards.

The Hidden Cellars line includes nine wines in a typical year. The Chevrignon d'Or, a dessert wine, has chalked up many of the winery's growing list of awards.

1500 Ruddick-Cunningham Road
Ukiah, CA 95482
(707) 462 0301

HOURS: 11 A.M.–4 P.M. daily,
    June–October; weekends only, the
    rest of the year
TASTINGS: Yes
TOURS: Yes
PICNIC AREA: Yes
RETAIL SALES: Yes
DIRECTIONS: From Highway 101 south of
    Ukiah, exit at Talmage; south on
    Ruddick-Cunningham Road.
AUTHOR'S CHOICE: Chevrignon d'Or

1987

Hidden Cellars

MENDOCINO COUNTY
JOHANNISBERG RIESLING
POTTER VALLEY

PRODUCED & BOTTLED BY HIDDEN CELLARS WINERY • UKIAH, CA
707-462-0301 • ALCOHOL 11.6% BY VOLUME • CONTAINS SULFITES

Olson Vineyards

Redwood Valley

First-time visitors who make the ten-minute trek up into the hills outside of Ukiah for the sole purpose of sampling the wines of Olson Vineyards are treated to an unexpected bonus. The Olsons serve their wine with a view that any other vintner would be hard pressed to match. The family home, which houses the tasting room, is situated on benchland overlooking Lake Mendocino and Redwood Valley.

Don Olson, a transplanted Los Angeles electronic engineer, moved his wife, Nancy and son, Dave, north to this site in 1971. The father-son winemaking team released the first Olson label vintage in 1983. Most of their grapes had previously been sold to Fetzer Winery.

The Olson establishment is a modest one. A wood-sided building next to the home shelters much of the operation. The crusher sits under an eave on the far side of the building, along with the press and wine tanks.

Although the pleasing view from the tasting room isn't for sale, it is for rent. An adjacent lake-view suite of downstairs rooms and a private deck are available to overnight guests on a bed-and-breakfast lodging plan. For those intending a shorter visit, the Olsons have set up picnic tables in their backyard, which also overlooks the lake.

3620 Road B
Redwood Valley, CA 95470
(707) 485-7523

HOURS: 10 A.M.–5 P.M. Thursday–Monday
TASTINGS: Yes
TOURS: Yes
PICNIC AREA: Yes
RETAIL SALES: Yes
DIRECTIONS: From Highway 101, east on Highway 20, north on Road A, then east on Road B.
VINTNER'S CHOICE: Special Reserve Zinfandel

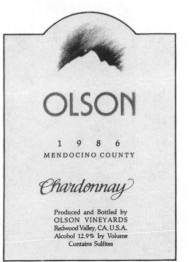

OLSON
1 9 8 6
MENDOCINO COUNTY
Chardonnay
Produced and Bottled by
OLSON VINEYARDS
Redwood Valley, CA, U.S.A.
Alcohol 12.9% by Volume
Contains Sulfites

Navarro Vineyards

Philo

Ted Bennett, founder of the Pacific Stereo chain, left the Bay Area in 1975 with his wife, Deborah Cahn, to establish Navarro Vineyards, a quaint winemaking operation in the Anderson Valley just north of Philo.

If the Navarro name is unfamiliar, it's probably because you'll not find the product in more than ten stores. About 80 percent of Navarro's 12,000 annual cases are sold from the tasting room, which, with its distinctively rustic style, is itself a lure to potential customers. Its arched windows and glass doors offer views of surrounding flowers and vines; an attached deck holds umbrella-shaded picnic tables.

Other similarly styled buildings on the property include the owner's home, which used to be a barn, and a small winery built around some old oak trees. Those who make prior arrangements with Ted and Deborah may tour the production and aging facilities.

Navarro produces estate-bottled Gewürztraminer, Chardonnay, and Pinot Noir. Small lots of grapes from other Mendocino County vineyards are used to make White Riesling, Cabernet Sauvignon, and an Edelwicker White Table Wine.

5601 Highway 128
Philo, CA 95466
(707) 895-3686
(800) 537-9463

HOURS: 10 A.M.–5 P.M. in winter;
    10 A.M.–6 P.M. in summer
TASTINGS: Yes
TOURS: By appointment
PICNIC AREA: Yes
RETAIL SALES: Yes
DIRECTIONS: Between Navarro and Philo
    on Highway 128.
VINTNER'S CHOICE: Gewürztraminer

ANDERSON VALLEY, MENDOCINO
Gewürztraminer
1986
ESTATE
DRY
BOTTLED

NAVARRO
Vineyards
PRODUCED & BOTTLED BY NAVARRO VINEYARDS
5601 HWY 128, PHILO, CA. CONTAINS SULFITES.
Alcohol 12.9% by volume. Telephone (707) 895-3686

Husch Vineyards

Philo

Husch is the oldest of the smattering of small wineries that occupy Mendocino County's cool Anderson Valley. While it is the elder, Husch is by no means old. Tony and Gretchen Husch bonded the operation in 1971.

Hugo Oswald and his family, who have grown grapes in Mendocino County for more than two decades, now own Husch, a 20,000-case-per-year winery situated between Navarro and Philo on Highway 128.

"Unadorned rustic" is how the Oswalds describe their facilities, which consist of a small, wood-frame winery and an old granary. The latter building now functions as a tasting room. Arbor-shaded picnic tables are available for visitors.

"La Ribera," the Oswald ranch near Ukiah, supplies a good portion of the winery's grapes. It is the Husch vineyard, however, that earned for the winery a bit of international fame. The 1983 estate-bottled Gewürztraminer was among a few California wines to accompany President Ronald Reagan on his trip to China in 1984. The Husch wine was served at a state dinner in Beijing in honor of People's Republic Premier Zhao Ziyang. Quite an honor for a wine that retailed at the time for just over six dollars per bottle.

4400 Highway 128
Philo, CA 95466
(707) 895-3216

HOURS: 10 A.M.–5 P.M. in winter;
   10 A.M.–6 P.M. in summer
TASTINGS: Yes
TOURS: By appointment
PICNIC AREA: Yes
RETAIL SALES: Yes
DIRECTIONS: Between Navarro and Philo
   on Highway 128.
VINTNER'S CHOICE: Chardonnay

ESTATE BOTTLED
HUSCH
LA RIBERA VINEYARDS

1986
MENDOCINO
SAUVIGNON BLANC

GROWN, PRODUCED AND BOTTLED BY THE H.A. OSWALD FAMILY
PHILO, MENDOCINO COUNTY, CA   ALCOHOL 13.1% BY VOLUME

THE NAPA VALLEY REGION

Leave the Crowds Behind

Psst! It's still possible to enjoy a leisurely tour of Napa Valley–area wineries. While the weekend congestion along narrow Highway 29 can often rival Los Angeles rush-hour traffic, a little planning and a sense of adventure will take you into a wonderland overlooked by all but the most seasoned winery enthusiasts.

The tours outlined in the following pages cover a wide area— from Green Valley, near the junction of Highways 80 and 680, all the way to Calistoga. In between are pleasant mountain roads and panoramic vistas that most wine country visitors pass up in favor of the more famous establishments on the valley floor.

The back roads of this region, while free of heavy traffic, are remarkably rich in wineries. Many have operated in relative obscurity for decades, their stately stone cellars visibly enhanced by age. Nichelini Vineyards, for example, has been in the same family since the mining days of the nineteenth century.

Others, like Chateau de Leu near Suisun in tiny Green Valley, are more recent additions to this world-famous countryside.

There is a common denominator, however. Each of these backroad operations welcomes visitors in an unhurried, intimate atmosphere that has all but disappeared from many of the larger wineries of Napa Valley. Just don't tell too many people.

Spending the night?

In St. Helena, the Wine Country Inn, a contemporary inn fashioned after hostelries of New England. I'm convinced my room that looked out over the valley (#24) was one of the finest in the region. A filling continental breakfast is served every morning. 1152 Lodi Lane, St. Helena, CA 94574; (707) 963-7077.

SUISUN TO RUTHERFORD

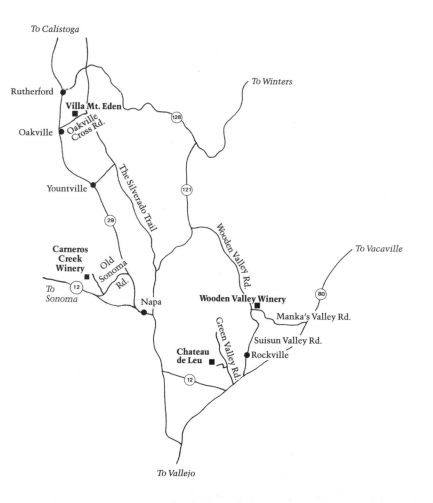

To Calistoga

To Winters

Rutherford

Villa Mt. Eden ■

Oakville Cross Rd.

Oakville

128

The Silverado Trail

121

Yountville

29

To Vacaville

Carneros Creek Winery ■

Old Sonoma Rd.

Wooden Valley Rd.

12

To Sonoma

Napa

80

Wooden Valley Winery ■

Manka's Valley Rd.

Green Valley Rd.

Suisun Valley Rd.

Chateau de Leu ■

Rockville

12

To Vallejo

Wooden Valley Winery

Suisun

During my visit to the Lanza family winery on Suisun Valley Road, a steady stream of customers pulled in to load their vehicles with supplies of Wooden Valley wines. That scene sufficiently explained the family's unusual independence. Other than the winery itself, a handful of restaurants are the only places one can order the Lanza product.

Wooden Valley Winery is a nondescript collection of older buildings that includes the home of the proprietors, the Lanza family. Lena and the late Mario Lanza bought Wooden Valley and more than 150 acres of vineyard from some friends back in the 1950s. In those days Suisun Valley Road was known as Wooden Valley Road; hence the name. Son Richard currently heads the family corporation, with assistance from his own four sons.

The family receives visitors at a long L-shaped bar in the spacious tasting room. The winery needs the space to display its wares. On my visit, the roster listed more than forty varieties. In addition to a traditional list of varietals, Wooden Valley produces Pink Chateau, Malvasia Bianca, four types of Sherry, Vermouth, and Champagne. The Lanzas bottle under the Wooden Valley, Solano, and Mario Lanza labels.

4756 Suisun Valley Road
Suisun, CA 94585
(707) 864-0730

HOURS: 9 A.M.–5 P.M. Tuesday–Sunday
TASTINGS: Yes
TOURS: No
PICNIC AREA: Yes
RETAIL SALES: Yes
DIRECTIONS: From Interstate 80 at Cordelia, north on Suisun Valley Road for 4.5 miles.
AUTHOR'S CHOICE: Malavasia Bianca

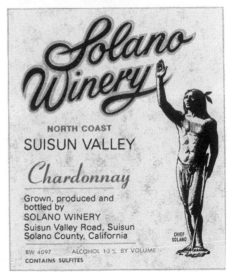

74 *Chateau de Leu*

Chateau de Leu

Green Valley–Suisun

A full century elapsed between the first plantings and the establishment of a winery in Green Valley, a tiny viticultural area where grapes have grown since 1882. The father and son team of Ben Volkhardt, Jr., and Ben III built Chateau de Leu in 1982 on land that has been owned by the family since the 1950s.

The family decided to create wines under their own label in 1981, after several years of selling grapes to other vintners. The result is an imposing French Tudor–style chateau designed to produce up to 25,000 cases per year.

The modern winery houses ten large temperature-controlled stainless steel fermentation tanks and scores of French Limousin barrels. Chateau de Leu also utilizes a field crusher that yields a thousand gallons per cycle.

Tours are by appointment, but a tasting room is open daily. This handsome public room is located on the second level and features a deck from which visitors can view Green Valley.

The four-square-mile basin gives way to mountains in all directions but south, allowing marine air off San Francisco Bay to interact with the region's own climatic conditions, thus producing grapes with a unique set of characteristics. Some 400 acres of Green Valley are presently planted to grapes.

1635 West Mason Road
Green Valley–Suisun, CA 94585
(707) 864-1517

HOURS: 11 A.M.–4:30 P.M. daily
TASTINGS: Yes
TOURS: By appointment
PICNIC AREA: Yes
RETAIL SALES: Yes
DIRECTIONS: Leave Interstate 80 at the Green Valley Road exit, north on Green Valley Road for 2 miles, left on West Mason, 1 mile to winery.
VINTNER'S CHOICE: Chardonnay

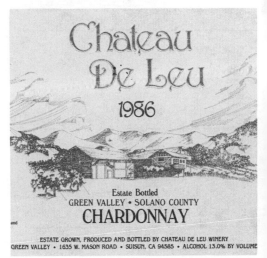

Carneros Creek Winery

Napa

A quest to develop "the perfect Pinot Noir" was progressing nicely when I dropped by Carneros Creek Winery, outside Napa.

A love of the great French Burgundies brought vintner Francis Mahoney to the Carneros region, where he found soil (rocky, clay loam) and climate (cooling breezes off San Pablo Bay) conditions similar to those in Burgundy. In 1973, he and partner Balfour Gibson broke ground for the first new winery in the Carneros region since Prohibition.

Reasoning that mediocre fruit was partly to blame for inferior California Pinot Noirs, Mahoney set about selecting the right "clones" to complement the geography and weather. The first clonal plot of Pinot Noir was established in 1975, and another several acres were planted a decade later. Much of the research into perfecting the grape was undertaken in conjunction with the University of California, Davis, where Mahoney studied enology.

While extremely proud of his carefully crafted Carneros Pinot Noir, Mahoney will undoubtedly be fine tuning his clones for years to come. In the meantime, those who make the trek out of Napa to visit the ivy-covered winery are welcomed by a friendly staff eager to share the continuing story of the "Pinot pioneer."

1285 Dealy Lane
Napa, CA 94559
(707) 253-WINE

HOURS: 9 A.M.–5 P.M. Wednesday–Sunday; Monday and Tuesday by appointment
TASTINGS: Yes
TOURS: By appointment
PICNIC AREA: Yes
RETAIL SALES: Yes
DIRECTIONS: From Highway 29 south of Napa, west on Highway 121/12. Right on Old Sonoma Road and left on Dealy Lane; 1 mile to winery.
VINTNER'S CHOICE: Pinot Noir

Villa Mt. Eden

Oakville

Villa Mt. Eden has operated on a century-old Napa Valley wine estate under various names and out of the public eye. Only in recent years has it begun to shed some of its mystery. The winery, while still maintaining a relatively low profile, has opened a tasting room for valley visitors and invites tours on a call-ahead basis. The estate belongs to James McWilliams and his wife, Anne, granddaughter of Bank of America founder A. P. Giannini.

The McWilliamses, who took over in 1970, obviously take pride in the estate, which is lovingly maintained. The winery buildings, one of which dates back to 1882, are painted white with blue trim. A rambling, 1920s-era Mediterranean-style villa serves as a weekend and summer retreat for the owners, who make their permanent home in San Francisco.

The several buildings, including an old pump house, form a tight cluster under an ancient eucalyptus tree. Tastings take place near the public entrance in a small converted home that also serves as an office. Clark Gable and Carole Lombard reportedly spent time at the little house while filming a movie on the property.

The eighty-seven acres of vines that encircle the winery extend to the Silverado Trail. The owners concentrate their efforts on Cabernet Sauvignon, Chardonnay, and Chenin Blanc.

Mt. Eden Ranch
620 Oakville Crossroad
P.O. Box 350
Oakville, CA 94562
(707) 944-8431

HOURS: 10 A.M.–4 P.M. daily; closed major holidays
TASTINGS: Yes
TOURS: By appointment
PICNIC AREA: Yes
RETAIL SALES: Yes
DIRECTIONS: On north side of Oakville Crossroad, which runs between the Silverado Trail and Highway 29.
VINTNER'S CHOICE: Cabernet Sauvignon

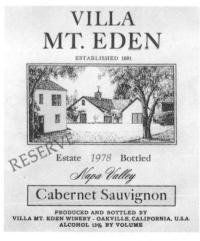

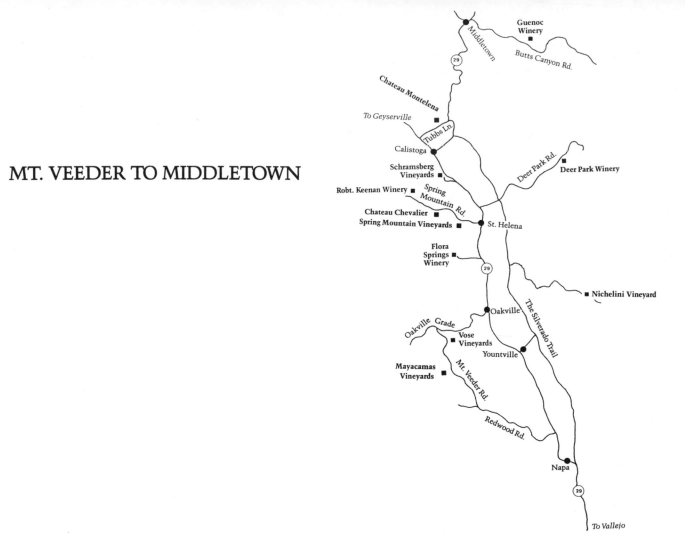

MT. VEEDER TO MIDDLETOWN

Guenoc
Winery

Middletown

Butts Canyon Rd.

Chateau Montelena

To Geyserville

Tubbs Ln.

Calistoga

Deer Park Rd.

Deer Park Winery

Schramsberg
Vineyards

Robt. Keenan Winery

Spring
Mountain Rd.

Chateau Chevalier
Spring Mountain Vineyards

St. Helena

Flora
Springs
Winery

Nichelini Vineyard

Oakville

The Silverado Trail

Oakville Grade

Vose
Vineyards

Yountville

Mayacamas
Vineyards

Mt. Veeder Rd.

Redwood Rd.

Napa

29

To Vallejo

80

Mt. Veeder to Middletown

Mayacamas Vineyards

Napa

One of the few California wineries whose vines are dusted with winter snows, Mayacamas Vineyards sits high in the mountains above the bustle of Napa and Sonoma valleys. The winery and vineyards are perched on an ancient volcanic ledge whose rich soil has fed the vines since German-born sword engraver John Fisher established his winemaking operation here in the late 1800s.

Bob and Nonie Travers are the present owners. The couple bought Mayacamas in 1968 after Bob left his job as a stock analyst in San Francisco. With the exception of the addition of a cellar and some new vines, Bob has done little to alter the rustic appearance of Mayacamas. Built into a hillside to take advantage of gravity, before the era of electric pumps, the old winery houses its crusher and press on the uppermost level. From there the juices flow into the original concrete-lined fermentation tanks. The Cabernets are aged in large American oak and small French oak barrels in the old stone-walled cellar below. While the Chardonnay is ready for consumption after three years of aging, patience is the key to enjoying Mayacamas reds. Bob uses winemaking techniques that give his Cabernets longevity and require a lengthier maturing time. "Prime enjoyment of our 1979 Cabernet Sauvignon should come in the last few years of this century and the first few of the next," he says. "We make red wine this way primarily, of course, to test the patience and restraint of our customers."

For those unwilling to wait until the year 2000 to taste the fruits of Mayacamas, the Traverses each year release a number of cases from a decade or so earlier.

Patience is also required of those who venture up the mountain roads to the winery. After navigating the eight or so miles of winding roads from Napa on the valley floor, visitors—and their vehicles—must endure a mile-long dirt driveway before reaching Mayacamas.

1155 Lokoya Road
Napa, CA 94558
(707) 224-4030

HOURS: By appointment
TASTINGS: No
TOURS: 10 A.M. Monday and Wednesday and 2 P.M. Friday, by appointment
PICNIC AREA: No
RETAIL SALES: By appointment
DIRECTIONS: Leave Highway 29 at Redwood Road, right on Mt. Veeder, left on Lokoya, left on dirt road at sign to winery.
VINTNER'S CHOICE: Cabernet Sauvignon

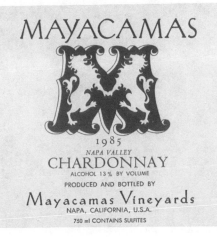

Vose Vineyards

Napa

Far above the madding Napa Valley crowds, vintner Hamilton Vose III quietly goes about his craft, interrupted only by the occasional visitor to his rustic mountain winemaking retreat.

The Vose compound, whose inhabitants include French frogs, squirrels, deer, and even a bear or mountain lion now and again, has expanded since the first vines were planted up here in 1973. In fact, the winery has welcomed visitors only since the mid 1980s, when Vose constructed a rambling redwood vista deck and gazebo, a site often used for weddings.

The first Vose wine, a 1977 White Zinfandel bearing the name Zinblanca, has earned an unusual reputation as "the" wine to enjoy with, believe it or not, popcorn. The winery even sells gift sets of wine and Indian popcorn. Other Vose creations include estate Chardonnay, estate Cabernet Sauvignon, estate Zinfandel, Gewürztraminer, and Fumé Blanc. Current annual production is about 25,000 cases.

Although he's been a vintner for well over a decade, Vose tried his hand at a few trades before the lure of the grape brought him to the slopes of Mt. Veeder. His previous occupations ran the proverbial gamut, from professional race driver and Naval underwater explosives expert to salesman and paper company executive.

If you're visiting the Napa Valley on a busy weekend, consider structuring an itinerary that targets Vose at lunchtime. The winery deck provides a perfect spot for a picnic and affords one of the valley's most unique and unobstructed views.

4035 Mt. Veeder Road
Napa, CA 94558
(707) 944-2254

HOURS: 11 A.M.–4 P.M. daily, May–November; by appointment December–April
TASTINGS: Weekends
TOURS: By appointment
PICNIC AREA: Yes
RETAIL SALES: Yes
DIRECTIONS: From Highway 29 at Oakville, west on Oakville Grade and left on Mt. Veeder Road for 2 miles. Winery is on the left.
AUTHOR'S CHOICE Zinblanca

Flora Springs Winery
St. Helena

Believe it or not, it's still possible to find a backroad winery or two in busy Napa Valley. Situated on the western edge of the valley at the end of a quiet country lane, Flora Springs is one of few wineries in the region where visitors can linger in an uncrowded, unhurried environment.

Jerry and Flora Komes discovered the neglected Martini family winery while scouting for a retirement haven back in the mid 1970s. The Komes' original plan involved using the 50-acre vineyard to help support their golden years. However, when their vision expanded to include producing premium wines, son John and daughter Julie, along with their own young families, joined the fold to help nurse the old winery back to a productive life.

Since then, the family has added 300 acres of new vineyard and rehabilitated the century-old stone winery. In the process, they've created a line of award-winning wines.

About the only magic the Flora Springs clan hasn't performed is an exorcism. It seems the old establishment was once included in a book as one of the Napa area's "ghost wineries." Hardly suited to that rather dubious honor these days, Flora Springs is a surviving example of what a few green thumbs and lots of elbow grease can do. It's no place for a self-respecting ghost anymore.

1978 West Zinfandel Lane
St. Helena, CA 94574
(707) 963-5711

HOURS: 10 A.M.–4 P.M. Monday–Saturday, by appointment
TASTINGS: By appointment
TOURS: By appointment
PICNIC AREA: By appointment
RETAIL SALES: By appointment
DIRECTIONS: From Highway 29 south of St. Helena, west on Zinfandel Lane; right after 1 mile at fork in road.
VINTNER'S CHOICE: Trilogy (a proprietary blend)

A NAPA VALLEY
RED TABLE WINE

TRILOGY
1984

A classic blend
of three traditional
claret varietals
specially selected
for this bottling

Flora Springs

Estate Grown, Produced and Bottled by
Flora Springs Wine Co. St. Helena, CA

Spring Mountain Vineyards

St. Helena

2805 Spring Mountain Road
St. Helena, CA 94574
(707) 963-5233

HOURS: 10 A.M.–4 P.M. daily
TASTINGS: Yes
TOURS: 10:30 A.M. and 2:30 P.M., by
    appointment
PICNIC AREA: No
RETAIL SALES: Yes
DIRECTIONS: From Highway 29 in St.
    Helena, west on Madrona, right on
    Spring Mountain Road for 1 mile to
    white gate and stone wall.
VINTNER'S CHOICES: Cabernet Sauvignon
    and Chardonnay

Wineries that are fortunate enough to earn a loyal following do so for their particular wares. One Napa Valley exception, however, is Spring Mountain Vineyard, which has come by its reputation not so much for its fine wines but for the manor house that has been seen by millions of television viewers.

Those who are not devotees of prime-time soap opera will probably be confused by all the fuss over a house. Followers of *Falcon Crest*, on the other hand, drive up by the hundreds each week to gawk at the stately Victorian that is featured in opening scenes of the TV show. First-time visitors will discover that the home is not included on the tour. This isn't a cause for disappointment, since the winery itself is one of the most handsome to be found in the region.

The above-ground portion of Spring Mountain Winery is fairly new, built by founder Michael Robbins in 1976 in a grand style similar to that of his Victorian residence a few hundred yards away. Inside are a richly appointed tasting room and upstairs offices. Stained glass, much of it designed and constructed by Robbins, is used generously throughout the public areas. A huge chandelier, which originally hung in the mansion, is now a fixture of the winery. A nice view of the house from the tasting area is framed by an arched window with etchings of grapevines.

Wines are aged in a long, century-old tunnel that was dug into the hillside behind the facility. An adjacent area is reserved for fermentation tanks.

In addition to the Spring Mountain label, the winery bottles a selection of wines under the name *Falcon Crest*. These wines, while not up to the premium standards of the Spring Mountain vintages, are nonetheless big sellers—for obvious reasons.

(At 3101 Spring Mountain Road is one of the most striking neighboring wineries: Chateau Chevalier. Though closed and for sale at this writing, a drive-by just to see this charmer through your windshield is worth the effort.)

Spring Mountain's
FALCON CREST.
1981
Napa Valley Gamay Beaujolais

PRODUCED AND BOTTLED BY SPRING MOUNTAIN VINEYARDS B.W. 4521
ST. HELENA, CALIFORNIA, U.S.A. ALCOHOL 12.4% BY VOLUME

Robert Keenan Winery

St. Helena

3660 Spring Mountain Road
St. Helena, CA 94574
(707) 963-9177

HOURS: Monday–Saturday, by
  appointment
TASTINGS: By appointment
TOURS: By appointment
PICNIC AREA: Yes
RETAIL SALES: Yes
DIRECTIONS: From Highway 29 in St.
  Helena, west on Madrona and right
  on Spring Mountain Road, 4.5 miles
  to winery lane, right 1 mile to
  winery.
VINTNER'S CHOICE: Merlot

I thought that I'd stumbled onto quite a discovery when I finally found my way out of St. Helena past deer, foxes, and rabbits to Robert Keenan Winery. But the hostess took the wind out of my sails when she noted that grapes had been grown up in these hills since the turn of the century. So much for discoveries.

Peter Conradi established these vineyards in 1892 and built the classic winery a dozen years later. The vineyards were abandoned some time ago, however, and deteriorated until Robert and Ann Keenan reclaimed the site from the forest, in 1974. He replanted nearly fifty acres of Cabernet Sauvignon, Chardonnay, and Merlot and set about completely refurbishing the old stone winery. The project was completed in time for the harvest of 1974.

The Keenan facility is a handsome, cozy, rustic affair, with stone walls, pitched roof, and lovely vineyard vistas. There's a gorgeous tasting area and dining room where, during my visit, a resident chef was turning out fine meals for Keenan visitors. Also available, to those who call ahead, are gourmet box lunches to enjoy on the scenic winery grounds.

By the way, a visit to the Keenan estate is certainly worth the cost of a car wash back in civilization. You'll definitely need it after leaving this backroad winery.

CABERNET SAUVIGNON
Napa Valley
1985
Produced and Bottled by
Robert Keenan Winery, Spring Mt. St. Helena, Ca.
CONTAINS SULFITES, ALCOHOL 13% BY VOLUME

Deer Park Winery

Deer Park

It is said that the Napa Valley is second only to Disneyland as California's biggest tourist attraction. You could fool David and Kinta Clark, however. Highway 29 traffic may be bumper to bumper most weekends, but the road up to the Clarks' little Deer Park Winery is usually pretty quiet.

Those who do venture out of St. Helena and are able to locate the winery will not be disappointed. The centerpiece at Deer Park is a rustic, century-old cellar that turns out wines in small amounts—only about 5,000 cases per year.

David is both winemaker and vineyard tender. When I visited Deer Park he was in the process of carving soil for additional vines, which would bring the total productive acreage to about six. The remaining forty or so acres on the property consist primarily of rocks, hills, and trees—nice to look at, but not conducive to cultivation.

David came by his winemaking talents through apprenticeships at Cuvaison and Clos du Val. He and Kinta, along with his sister and brother-in-law, Lila and Bob Knapp, bought Deer Park in 1979, resuming a tradition of winemaking that began in 1891 on the estate.

Like many old wineries built into hillsides, Deer Park was set up to operate on a gravity-flow basis. In the old days, wagons would unload the grapes at the top of the hill at the upper part of the building where crushing took place. Gravity carried the juices downhill to fermentation and aging cooperage. Although more modern means are used these days, David, for sentimental reasons, has held on to much of the equipment from Deer Park's earlier years.

The name indicates otherwise, but the Clarks say there are no deer at Deer Park. The way David tells it, the moniker was apparently conceived by a 1920s-era owner who wanted to shake any unpleasant association of his winery with the country byway that ends at the property—Sanitarium Road.

1000 Deer Park Road
Deer Park, CA 94576
(707) 963-5411

HOURS: 10 A.M.–4 P.M. daily, by appointment
TASTINGS: By appointment
TOURS: By appointment
PICNIC AREA: Yes, by appointment
RETAIL SALES: Yes
DIRECTIONS: From Highway 29 north of St. Helena, east on Deer Park Road for 3.5 miles to winery.
VINTNER'S CHOICE: Zinfandel

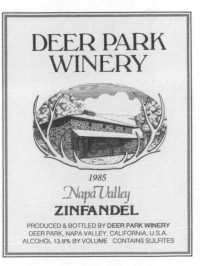

DEER PARK WINERY

1985
Napa Valley
ZINFANDEL

PRODUCED & BOTTLED BY DEER PARK WINERY
DEER PARK, NAPA VALLEY, CALIFORNIA, U.S.A.
ALCOHOL 13.8% BY VOLUME   CONTAINS SULFITES

Nichelini Vineyard

St. Helena

Antone Nichelini was among the group of Italian immigrants that worked the magnesite mines in the hills above Napa during the nineteenth century. When mining activity slowed, Nichelini homesteaded some land and, in 1890, built a modest sandstone winery topped by a home in which he raised his family.

The operation thrived until Prohibition, during which Nichelini reportedly maintained a clandestine winemaking business. Although Repeal signaled the reopening of wineries throughout the state, a bootlegging conviction precluded Antone from securing a license. His son, William, obtained the necessary permits and helped to keep the vineyard going through the ensuing ups and owns of the industry. When the price of whole grapes took a dive in the mid-1940s, William's seventeen-year-old son, Jim, (pictured here before his death in 1984) was recruited to help his father increase wine production.

Although the first three generations of Nichelini Vineyard proprietors are now gone, their contributions to the property are still evident. The original homesteader's cabin has been preserved, as has an old Roman press which was retired in the 1950s. Numerous other pieces of antiquated winery equipment and assorted odds and ends are on display here as well.

Today the winery is operated by Jim's daughter, Jo-Ann Nichelini-Meyer, who grew up here and apprenticed with her father before his death. With the number of family-owned wineries dwindling each year, the Nichelini story is fast becoming the exception in California winemaking.

2950 Sage Canyon Road (Highway 128)
St. Helena, CA 94574
(707) 963-3357

HOURS: 10 A.M.–6 P.M. Saturday and
    Sunday; weekdays by appointment
TASTINGS: Yes
TOURS: Yes, self-guided
PICNIC AREA: Yes
RETAIL SALES: Yes
DIRECTIONS: Eleven miles east of
    Highway 29 on Sage Canyon Road
    (Highway 128)
VINTNER'S CHOICE: Zinfandel

Nichelini
VINEYARD
PRIVATE   RESERVE

Founded 1890

NAPA VALLEY
CABERNET
SAUVIGNON

PRODUCED AND BOTTLED BY JAMES E. NICHELINI
BONDED WINERY NO. 843, ST. HELENA, CALIFORNIA
ALCOHOL 12½% BY VOLUME

Schramsberg Vineyards

Calistoga

Jack and Jamie Davies probably asked themselves, more than once, "What have we gotten into?" when they purchased the rundown Schramsberg wine estate back in 1965. If it hadn't been for their determination, we probably wouldn't be enjoying Schramsberg Champagnes today.

The winery, one of the state's oldest, got off to a rousing start. Established in 1862 by German immigrant Jacob Schram, the winery was featured prominently in Robert Louis Stevenson's book *Silverado Squatters*, published a century ago. However, the death of Schram, the onset of Prohibition, and the ravages of phylloxera dealt a near-terminal blow to the historic property. Enter the Davies.

Formerly an executive with several large companies and a graduate of Harvard, Jack enlisted the support of his wife, Jamie, and rehabilitated and reactivated Schramsberg. Their first crush came in 1966.

Since then, the couple has regularly introduced new names to the Schramsberg wine roster, and they recently purchased the adjacent McEachran Winery estate in order to expand their winemaking business.

You'll need an appointment to visit this California Historical Society Landmark, which sits among the trees a couple of miles south of Calistoga.

1400 Schramsberg Road
Calistoga, CA 94515
(707) 942-4558

HOURS: Monday–Saturday, by appointment
TASTINGS: By appointment
TOURS: By appointment
PICNIC AREA: No
RETAIL SALES: By appointment
DIRECTIONS: West off Highway 29 (5 miles north of St. Helena) on Peterson Drive, quick right onto private road, up the hill to winery.
AUTHOR'S CHOICE: Blanc de Noir

Schramsberg
FOUNDED 1862

CUVÉE DE PINOT

NAPA VALLEY
CHAMPAGNE

BRUT ROSÉ 1985
PINOT NOIR

PRODUCED AND BOTTLED BY
SCHRAMSBERG VINEYARDS
CALISTOGA, CALIFORNIA

ALCOHOL 12% BY VOLUME
CONTAINS SULFITES
CONTENTS 750 MLS

Chateau Montelena

Calistoga

Divergent influences of Chinese and French architecture stand side by side at one of Napa Valley's oldest and most intriguing small wineries.

Chateau Montelena was built in 1882 by California State Senator and prominent Bay Area businessman Alfred Tubbs. In establishing his winery near the base of Mount St. Helena, Senator Tubbs called upon the design talents of an architect from France who created a building in the style of a French chateau. The medieval facade was fashioned from imported cut stone. The other walls—the winery is cut into the side of a hill—are as thick as twelve feet in certain places, providing an environment akin to a cave, perfect for making wine.

While the winery itself conjures up images of feudal Bordeaux, the adjacent grounds could have been lifted from a garden in Peking. Jade Lake, with its delicate tea houses, graceful bridges, and an old Chinese junk, was added to the property by the Yort Franks, later owners who in the 1950s created a living reminder of their ancestral homeland, China.

The latest chapter in the Montelena story is being written by a partnership that took over in 1972. The new owners have preserved the architectural heritage of the winery and nurtured the gardens while carving a new reputation for their product. This winemaking renaissance is evidenced in part by framed menus from the White House that list Montelena wines. These hang in the tasting room along with other awards bestowed on the chateau's wines in recent years.

Chateau Montelena produces Cabernet Sauvignon, Chardonnay, Johannisberg Riesling, and Zinfandel.

1429 Tubbs Lane
Calistoga, CA 94515
(707) 942-5105

HOURS: 10 A.M.–4 P.M. daily
TASTINGS: Yes
TOURS: 11 A.M. and 2 P.M., by appointment
PICNIC AREA: By appointment
RETAIL SALES: Yes
DIRECTIONS: From Highway 29, east on Tubbs Lane to winery gate.
VINTNER'S CHOICE: Cabernet Sauvignon

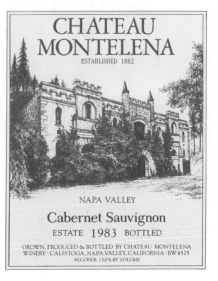

Guenoc Winery

Middletown

Unless you're a history buff, you probably wouldn't recognize the visage of English stage actress Lillie Langtry that adorns the Guenoc Winery label. Lillie, it seems, not only enthralled audiences in the late 1800s but had at least a passing fancy for wine. When she wasn't hobnobbing with British royalty or touring the world's stages, the lovely ingenue known as "Jersey Lily" relaxed at her spacious country house and vineyards in the Guenoc Valley, near Clear Lake.

Lillie's stately white home is now part of the Guenoc Winery estate in the nation's first government-approved grape-growing region, or appellation, under single proprietorship. Orville Magoon, a coastal engineer turned grape-grower and winemaker, owns the 270-acre spread, which also features a modern, 54,000-square-foot winery.

Visitors are invited to sample Guenoc wines (Sauvignon Blanc, Chardonnay, Cabernet Sauvignon, Petite Sirah, Zinfandel, and Merlot) but unfortunately are unable to tour the Langtry house. However, the veranda-bedecked home can be seen from the winery. Guests are invited to picnic under arbors overlooking the lovely hills and lake.

21000 Butts Canyon Road
Middletown, CA 95461
(707) 987-2385

HOURS: 10 A.M.–4:30 P.M. Thursday–Sunday; closed major holidays
TASTINGS: Yes
TOURS: Yes
PICNIC AREA: Yes
RETAIL SALES: Yes
DIRECTIONS: From Calistoga, north on Highway 29 to Middletown, right at "Guenoc Valley" sign onto Butts Canyon Road; 6 miles to winery.
VINTNER'S CHOICE: Cabernet Sauvignon

Guenoc

1986
Lake County 58%
Napa County 42%
Sauvignon Blanc

Produced and Bottled by Guenoc Winery
Middletown, California Alcohol 12.6% by Vol.

THE CENTRAL COAST

Cruising the Coastal Byways

I f your visits to the Central Coast have been confined to the popular seaside resorts, you'll be surprised at the growing list of wineries operating along the back roads of this region. A day trip from Santa Cruz, Monterey, Carmel, or San Jose will introduce you to several enticing winemaking operations and some of the state's most beautiful countryside.

The coastal scenery is diverse as well. If your starting point is the Monterey Peninsula, you'll quickly exchange the cool coastal environs for the warmer climate of Carmel Valley. After winding eastward to the top of the mountains, the fertile Salinas Valley unfolds below. This roller coaster tour culminates with a jaunt down the slope, a short hop across the valley floor, and a final ascent toward the Pinnacles National Monument above Soledad.

Equally impressive is the setting in and around Santa Cruz County, where golden beaches give way to redwood forests only a few miles inland.

If your tour route is Hecker Pass Road between Watsonville and Gilroy, be sure to include a visit to the less crowded wineries of the Uvas Valley. It is here that hospitable vintners like the Kirigin-Chargin (Kirigin Cellars) and the Parks (Sycamore Creek Vineyards) families practice the age-old art at two of the region's oldest and most charming wineries.

Free tour guides to Central Coast wineries are available from local chambers of commerce. For details, see the Grape Escapes section at the back of this book.

Spending the night?

In Pacific Grove, the Gosby House Inn, built in 1887. The old, comfy Victorian is a short walk from the ocean. Most rooms have private baths. 643 Lighthouse Avenue, Pacific Grove, CA 93950; (408) 375-1287.

In Santa Cruz, the Babbling Brook Inn. Twelve rooms with private decks, fireplaces, and private baths. 1025 Laurel Street, Santa Cruz, CA 95060; (408) 427-1766.

LOS GATOS TO IGNACIO

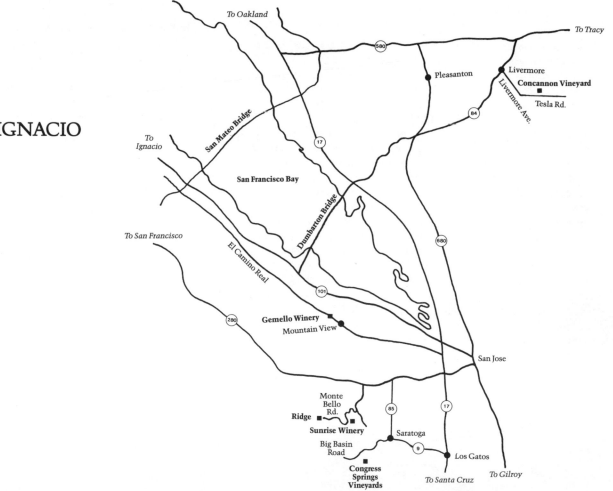

To Oakland

To Tracy

580

Pleasanton

Livermore

Concannon Vineyard

84

Livermore Ave.

Tesla Rd.

San Mateo Bridge

To
Ignacio

17

San Francisco Bay

Dumbarton Bridge

680

To San Francisco

El Camino Real

101

280

Gemello Winery

Mountain View

San Jose

Monte
Bello
Rd.

Ridge

85

17

Sunrise Winery

Saratoga

Big Basin
Road

9

Los Gatos

**Congress
Springs
Vineyards**

To Santa Cruz

To Gilroy

Congress Springs Vineyards

Saratoga

During the early years of Santa Cruz Mountains winemaking, the series of vineyards in this part of the range was known as the *Chaîne d'Or*, or "Golden Chain," for the acclaimed vintages and the region's beauty.

Part of the credit for the development of this area's wine industry goes to Pierre Pourroy, who left France in the 1800s and cleared redwood forestland to establish the first vineyards in what today is known as Congress Springs Vineyards.

Despite the wild growth of the Santa Clara Valley, Congress Springs, just outside quaint Saratoga, remains a tranquil, secluded spot that provides locals with a refuge from the daily high-tech grind.

The panoramic view from the winery itself is breathtaking. Too bad tasters aren't able to enjoy it along with a glass of Congress Springs wine. Wares are sampled in a long, windowless building downslope from the winery.

After a visit to the tasting room, we ambled up the road for a closer look at the winery-on-the-hill, built in the early 1920s and one of the valley's first all-cement structures. The vineyards over which "Villa de Monmarte" presides these days are rich and fruitful, although a scant decade or so ago the place was overgrown and forgotten. The Erickson and Gehrs families stepped in around 1976, rescuing the estate from more than twenty years of neglect.

Today, reinvigorated and well cared for, Congress Springs is one of the shining links in the coastal range's Golden Chain.

23600 Congress Springs Road
Saratoga, CA 95070
(408) 867-1409

HOURS: 11 A.M.–5 P.M. daily
TASTINGS: Yes
TOURS: By appointment
PICNIC AREA: Yes
RETAIL SALES: Yes
DIRECTIONS: Leave Saratoga on Big Basin Way (which turns into Congress Springs Road); 3 miles to winery drive.
AUTHOR'S CHOICE: Pinot Noir

CONGRESS SPRINGS

1987
Santa Clara County
CHARDONNAY

WHITE TABLE WINE

Sunrise Winery

Cupertino

Approaching the Picchetti winery for the first time, I halfway expected to encounter a grizzled old cowboy, a jug or two in hand, heading back to the bunkhouse.

California still holds a few surviving wineries from before the twentieth century. No other, however, retains quite the authentic flavor that has been preserved up here above Silicon Valley.

The Picchetti Ranch, now known as Sunrise Winery, exists in what might best be described as a state of arrested decay. It still functions well as a winery. But, though some of the 1870s-era compound has been updated (renovation is continuing), visitors encounter a scene that appears much like it must have back in the old days. The rickety outbuildings—replete with marble doorknobs, old wine bottles, and vintage winemaking and farming equipment—offer an authentic glimpse into another time.

Much like the state's efforts in preserving the Gold Rush burg of Columbia in the Mother Lode, the Midpeninsula Regional Open Space District stepped in to purchase 200,000 acres here back in the mid 1970s. The winery sat abandoned for several years. It has since been leased—for a reported one dollar per year—by Rolayne and Ronald Stortz. In exchange for the reasonable lease arrangement, the Stortz family has agreed to restore the old winery.

The Stortz clan resides in a stately Victorian downslope from the working part of the ranch. Tastings are conducted in the top level of the vintage, brick-walled winery.

Grapes for Sunrise wines come not only from the ranch but from vineyards in other north-state locales. Annual production is a modest 2,500 cases of Pinot Blanc, Chardonnay, White Riesling, Petite Sirah, Pinot Noir, Cabernet Sauvignon, and Sauvignon Blanc. The winery also produces an estate Zinfandel from ninety-year-old vines on the ranch.

13100 Montebello Road
Cupertino, CA 95014
(408) 741-1310

HOURS: 11 A.M.–3 P.M. Friday–Sunday; closed major holidays
TASTINGS: Yes
TOURS: By appointment
PICNIC AREA: Yes
RETAIL SALES: Yes
DIRECTIONS: From Interstate 280, southwest on Foothill Expressway for 3.5 miles, right on Montebello Road for .5 mile to winery lane.
VINTNER'S CHOICE: Pinot Noir and Pinot Blanc

SUNRISE

PRODUCED AND BOTTLED BY SUNRISE CELLARS
LIVERMORE, CALIFORNIA

1985
Santa Maria Valley
WHITE RIESLING
(Bien Nacido Vineyard)

Alcohol 11.7% by volume

Ridge

Cupertino

To the north, the skyscrapers of San Francisco's financial district are often visible. Below, the high technology capital of the world sprawls along the valley floor. As I drank the view with a glass of Ridge Zinfandel, the name Paradox Ridge seemed more suitable for this winery.

Even though computers have made their way into this internationally famous winemaking establishment, the unpretentious ranch scene that greets visitors at Ridge stands in ultimate contrast to Silicon Valley, more than 2,000 feet below.

That's part of the tradition at Ridge, where the "old ways" apply to both aesthetics and winemaking. The winery actually exists in two parts. The lower site—formerly the Torres Winery—houses offices, a tasting area, and case storage. The old Perrone Winery, a redwood and stone structure, is the actual production facility for Ridge wines and is not open to the public.

Ridge Vineyards is a relatively new name, originated in 1959 when four Stanford Research Institute scientists set up shop here, making wine with their families during spare moments. Ridge's reputation dates from the first release in 1962, but much of the winery's notoriety can be traced to the arrival of Paul Draper. The Stanford alumnus joined the operation as winemaker in 1969 after studying and practicing the trade in Italy, France, and Chile. Paul was among the first to popularize the claret-style Zinfandels that have since been widely emulated.

Ridge has fifty nonirrigated acres planted to grapes and makes purchases from various other vineyards whose appellations are noted on the labels. Annual production fluctuates between 30,000 and 40,000 cases, with Cabernet Sauvignon representing about 40 percent of the total. In addition to Zinfandel, Ridge produces a small amount of Petite Sirah.

17100 Montebello Road
Cupertino, CA 95015
(408) 867-3233

HOURS: 11 A.M.–3 P.M. Saturday
TASTINGS: Yes
TOURS: No
PICNIC AREA: Yes
RETAIL SALES: Yes
DIRECTIONS: From Highway 280, south on Foothill Boulevard, right on Montebello Road for 4.4 miles.
VINTNER'S CHOICE: Ridge Zinfandel

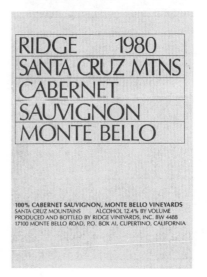

RIDGE 1980
SANTA CRUZ MTNS
CABERNET
SAUVIGNON
MONTE BELLO

100% CABERNET SAUVIGNON, MONTE BELLO VINEYARDS
SANTA CRUZ MOUNTAINS   ALCOHOL 12.4% BY VOLUME
PRODUCED AND BOTTLED BY RIDGE VINEYARDS, INC. BW 4488
17100 MONTE BELLO ROAD, P.O. BOX A1, CUPERTINO, CALIFORNIA

Gemello Winery

Mountain View

Upon visiting historic Gemello Winery in the midst of bustling Mountain View, guests often remark that the location is "a strange place for a winery." In truth, it's a strange place for a city, since Gemello was here long before the bowling alley, drive-in restaurant, and apartments that today squeeze the modest establishment. A house, tasting room/store and winery are all that remain of a once-sprawling winemaking operation that included more than two dozen acres of vineyard.

Gemello was founded just after Repeal by John Gemello, a native of Italy's Piemonte region. Settling with his family on a ranch overlooking the valley, John set about making robust red wines in an oak-aged style that is observed to this day at the winery. The winemaker helped dig the cellar next to an old apricot-drying room that was converted into a production facility.

John's son Mario took over some years later and operated the business until his retirement in 1978. There being no immediate family interest, crushing ceased, and much of the winery equipment was sold.

Several miles away in Half Moon Bay, however, John Gemello's granddaughter, Sandy, and her husband, Paul Obester, were in the early stages of establishing Obester Winery. In 1982, Sandy and Paul stepped in to carry on the Gemello tradition, and production resumed, on a smaller scale. The winery today bottles less than 5,000 cases per year.

Gemello is open only for special events (as announced in the winery newsletter), including a popular bring-your-own-bottle event held every couple of months. Using the winery's vintage equipment, customers fill their own containers with special Gemello blends.

2003 El Camino Real
Mountain View, CA 94040
Mailing address: 12341 San Mateo Road
Half Moon Bay, CA 94019
(415) 726-9463

HOURS: Open only on special occasions.
TASTINGS: On special occasions
TOURS: On special occasions
PICNIC AREA: No
RETAIL SALES: On special occasions
DIRECTIONS: From Highway 101, take Rengstorff exit south, left at El Camino Real to winery drive.
VINTNER'S CHOICES: Cabernet Sauvignon and White Zinfandel

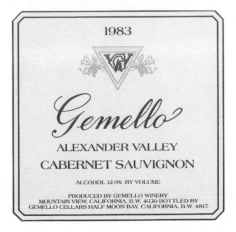

1983

Gemello

ALEXANDER VALLEY
CABERNET SAUVIGNON

ALCOHOL 12.9% BY VOLUME

PRODUCED BY GEMELLO WINERY
MOUNTAIN VIEW, CALIFORNIA. B.W. 4030 BOTTLED BY
GEMELLO CELLARS HALF MOON BAY, CALIFORNIA. B.W. 4817.

Concannon Vineyard

Livermore

James Concannon's pioneering efforts in the western wine industry were largely the result of urgings from a San Francisco archbishop who needed a reliable source of sacramental wines for the Catholic Church. The Irish immigrant obliged by purchasing forty-seven acres in 1883, establishing what is today one of the state's oldest continuously operating wineries.

James transcended the original intention of his winery, becoming well known to others outside the church. In searching for other grape-growing locales, he later took his talents to Mexico and is widely credited with establishing that country's wine industry.

The winery still produces sacramental wines but is better known these days for such varieties as Sauvignon Blanc, Cabernet Sauvignon, Chardonnay, and Livermore Riesling. Concannon was the first American winery to make Petite Sirah, which was released in 1964. Dr. Sergio Traverso is the new owner/winemaker.

A cavernous masonry facility that sits amid vineland at the edge of Livermore, the winery makes admirable efforts to accommodate visitors. Tours are given four times daily, and the tasting room is open seven days a week. Concannon's well-maintained grounds include several picnic tables scattered about an expansive lawn.

4590 Tesla Road
Livermore, CA 94550
(415) 447-3760

HOURS: 10 A.M.–4:30 P.M. Monday–Saturday; noon–4:30 P.M. Sunday
TASTINGS: Yes
TOURS: Four times daily
PICNIC AREA: Yes
RETAIL SALES: Yes
DIRECTIONS: From Interstate 580 (east), take North Livermore Avenue and drive south 3 miles to Tesla Road and winery.
VINTNER'S CHOICE: Petite Sirah

SELECTED 1986 VINEYARDS

Concannon
VINEYARD

CALIFORNIA

WHITE ZINFANDEL
WILSON VINEYARDS-CLARKSBURG

VINTED AND BOTTLED BY CONCANNON VINEYARD
LIVERMORE, CA   ALCOHOL 10.7% BY VOLUME

Pacheco Ranch Winery

Ignacio

It seems only logical that trendy Marin County, famous for hot tubs and BMWs, would have its own premium winery. Truth is, Pacheco Ranch was here long before wine—and Marin County, for that matter—were in vogue.

The estate is part of a large tract of land granted to Ignacio Pacheco in the early 1800s. In fact, Pacheco Ranch is still owned and maintained by Ignacio's direct descendants.

The old Pacheco Victorian, which sits adjacent to the winery, is the home of Frances Rowland, daughter-in-law of the late Abigail Telsfora Pacheco. Frances's son Herb, his wife, Debbie, and their children live in another house on the ranch. Herb and Debbie manage the operation and are assisted by Frances's daughter, Ann, and her winemaker husband, Jamie Meves.

According to Herb, whose weekday occupation is practicing law, great-grandfather Ignacio is believed to have planted the first grapevines in the area. Those early vines are gone, but Herb has carried on the family winemaking tradition by cultivating his own vineyards, beginning in 1970. The winery was bonded in 1979.

The Pacheco Ranch Winery, one of California's smallest, produces several hundred cases of 100 percent vintage Cabernet Sauvignon and about 500 cases of Chardonnay annually. Herb vows that any future growth won't exceed 5,000 cases. At Pacheco, good things come in small batches.

5495 Redwood Highway
Ignacio, CA 94947
(415) 883-5583

HOURS: By appointment
TASTINGS: By appointment
TOURS: By appointment
PICNIC AREA: No
RETAIL SALES: By appointment
DIRECTIONS: The winery sits west of Highway 101 in Ignacio, Marin County. Call for specific directions.
VINTNER'S CHOICE: Cabernet Sauvignon

PACHECO RANCH WINERY

1984

SONOMA COUNTY CHARDONNAY

PRODUCED & BOTTLED BY
PACHECO RANCH WINERY, IGNACIO, CA B.W. 4886
ALCOHOL 13.4% BY VOLUME

MORGAN HILL TO UVAS VALLEY

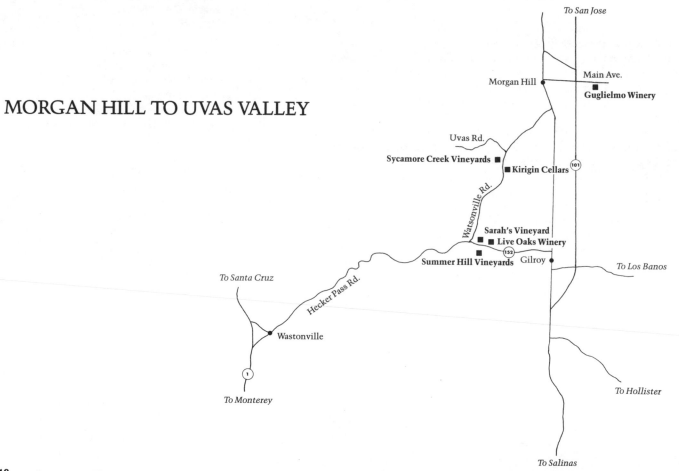

To San Jose

Main Ave.
Morgan Hill
■ **Guglielmo Winery**

Uvas Rd.
Sycamore Creek Vineyards ■
■ **Kirigin Cellars**

Watsonville Rd.

Sarah's Vineyard
■ **Live Oaks Winery**
■ **Summer Hill Vineyards**   Gilroy ●   To Los Banos

To Santa Cruz

Hecker Pass Rd.

Wastonville

To Monterey

To Hollister

To Salinas

Morgan Hill to the Uvas Valley

Emilio Guglielmo Winery

Morgan Hill

1480 East Main Avenue
Morgan Hill, CA 95037
(408) 779-2145

HOURS: 9 A.M.–5 P.M. Monday–Friday,
10 A.M.–5 P.M. Saturday and Sunday
TASTINGS: Yes
TOURS: By appointment
PICNIC AREA: Yes
RETAIL SALES: Yes
DIRECTIONS: One-and-a-half miles from
downtown Morgan Hill on East Main.
AUTHOR'S CHOICE: Brandy

It seemed only logical for George, Gene, and Gary Guglielmo to follow their father's footsteps into the winemaking business. After all, there must be at least a trace of wine in their blood. Since Roman times, when Guglielmos made wine in Northern Italy, traditions have been passed down from generation to generation.

The family history on this continent can be traced back three generations, to Emilio Guglielmo's arrival in the Santa Clara Valley in the early 1900s. He worked for more than a dozen years to earn enough money to buy fifteen acres, build a home, and establish a small basement winery. His dedication to the art and his years of experience were rewarded as Guglielmo wines became well known, particularly within San Francisco's French and Italian communities.

After weathering the devastating effects of Prohibition, Emilio and his son, George, expanded and modernized the winery. The operation has since passed to George's sons.

Although expansions and stucco have given the complex of buildings a more contemporary appearance, the atmosphere and charm of the old days have been retained. The old homestead is still here, and the basement still functions as part of the winery. Additions to the post-Repeal ivy-covered storage buildings have, at least in style, been consistent with the old structures. At the center of the grounds, a refurbished bunkhouse, sporting a new Tudor facade, serves as tasting room and offices.

In addition to its roster of more than a dozen varietals, Guglielmo bottles a line of premium table and specialty wines under the name Emile's. These include Champagne, Sherry, Vermouth, fruit wines, and Brandy.

Emile's
PRIVATE STOCK

CALIFORNIA
PREMIUM WHITE WINE

VINTED & BOTTLED BY EMILIO GUGLIELMO WINERY
MORGAN HILL, SANTA CLARA VALLEY, CA B.W. 3656
ALCOHOL 11% BY VOLUME   CONTAINS SULFITES

Sycamore Creek Vineyards

Morgan Hill

In contrast to their neighbor, Nikola Kirigin-Chargin of Kirigin Cellars, who has been making wine for most of his life, Terry and Mary Kaye Parks are the new kids on the block.

Former schoolteachers, the Parkses joined the "back-to-the-land" movement and bought an aging ranch in the Uvas Valley. After spending a few years fixing the place and dabbling in home winemaking, they learned that the nearby Marchetti Winery was for sale and went to take a look. "Terry fell in love with the place," recalled Mary Kaye.

The vines at Sycamore Creek are a mix of old and new. About half of the sixteen acres of vines date back to the early 1900s. The resulting wines–Carignane, Chardonnay, Johannisberg Riesling, and Sauvignon Blanc—have consistently won top honors in state competitons. The Parkses also purchase grapes from neighboring vineyards and from other California vineyards.

Sycamore Creek's many awards are displayed prominently behind the bar in the rustic tasting area, a converted hayloft inside the old winery barn. Large windows have been installed in the tasting loft to provide sweeping views of the creek, the vineyards, and the mountains beyond.

Because of the size of their operation—the annual capacity is 5,000 cases—the Parkses are able to give their wines a personal attention not possible at larger wineries. They are particularly proud of the fact that Sycamore Creek white wines are chemical free—fermented without the addition of SO_2.

The winery at Sycamore Creek is a family operation. Visitors are likely to find Terry and Mary Kaye behind the bar and at the controls of the bottling equipment. Even their two young sons pitch in.

While picnic facilities are not available at Sycamore Creek, Santa Clara County maintains a small picnic and rest area just a few miles away on Watsonville Road between the winery and Highway 152.

12775 Uvas Road
Morgan Hill, CA 95037
(408) 779-4738

HOURS: 11:30 A.M.–5 P.M. Saturday and Sunday
TASTINGS: Yes
TOURS: By appointment
PICNIC AREA: No
RETAIL SALES: Yes
DIRECTIONS: From Hecker Pass Road (Highway 152), north on Watsonville Road to Uvas Road Intersection.
VINTNER'S CHOICES: Zinfandel and Cabernet Sauvignon

Sycamore Creek
1982
California
ZINFANDEL
Estate Bottled
PRODUCED AND BOTTLED BY SYCAMORE CREEK VINEYARDS
MORGAN HILL, CALIFORNIA   ALCOHOL 13.0% BY VOLUME

Kirigin Cellars

Gilroy

The communist takeover of Croatia (now Yugoslavia) in 1945 spelled the end of the generations-old winemaking operation of the Kirigin-Chargin family. After the new government took over the winery, vintner Nikola Kirigin-Chargin decided to take his family and leave their homeland. "I could live without wine, but not without freedom," he said.

The family emigrated in 1959, and Kirigin-Chargin resumed his career in the United States, serving as winemaker at San Martin and Almaden wineries.

Kirigin-Chargin, who holds a degree in enology from the University of Zagreb, called upon his education and years of European and American wine-making experience in striking out on his own in the Uvas Valley of Santa Clara County. Housed in the old Bonesio Winery, which was established in 1833, Kirigin (pronounced Kuh-REE-gun) Cellars has, since 1976, successfully combined old world and modern winemaking technologies.

The equipment used by the winery is among the most modern to be found in this region, according to the winemaker. New 3,000-gallon stainless steel tanks hold the fermenting juices, while the clearing, maturing, and aging processes occur in redwood tanks and small oak barrels in Kirigin-Chargin's insulated cellar. The vats are contained in an old wooden bar that in recent years has been covered with tan-colored stucco.

In addition to the more than one dozen red and white varietals, Kirigin Cellars markets dessert wines, including a Vin de Mocca, which carries a rich coffee flavor.

Visitors to Kirigin Cellars enter the unassuming, dimly lit tasting room through a door fashioned from a weathered wine barrel. The room sits behind the family residence, a grand old home once owned by millionaire Henry Miller, a turn-of-the-century cattle baron. Though the Millers lived in high style, Kirigin-Chargin and his wife enjoy a simpler existence. "I bought this winery for pleasure," he said. "At my age, to think I'll become rich is foolish."

11550 Watsonville Road
Gilroy, CA 95020
(408) 847-8827

HOURS: 9 A.M.–6 P.M. daily
TASTINGS: Yes
TOURS: By appointment
PICNIC AREA: Yes
RETAIL SALES: Yes
DIRECTIONS: From Hecker Pass Road (Highway 152), north on Watsonville Road.
VINTNER'S CHOICE: Kirigin-Chargin doesn't enter wine competitions and refuses to acknowledge a favorite. "I like all my wines," he says.

Sarah's Vineyard

Gilroy

A honking gaggle of geese sounded my arrival at Sarah's Vineyard, a tiny Hecker Pass winemaking operation bonded in 1978. The name is a figment of the imagination of winemaker Marilyn Otteman, who, with husband John, owns and operates the establishment that despite its young age is earning a statewide reputation for its Chardonnay.

"A winery must have at least two personnel," John told me. "A winemaker and a hose dragger. I'm the hose dragger." The couple met some years ago while Marilyn was working at a home winemaking store in Southern California. Together, they built Sarah's, an immaculate little redwood-sided winery that sits on the side of a hill just under the Otteman home.

Visitors park at the end of a long driveway off Highway 152 and walk a few hundred yards through Chardonnay vineyards to the winery—along with the escort of geese, who share the property with assorted other animals.

The vineyard at Sarah's consists of seven acres, all Chardonnay, planted in 1980 by friends whose names are immortalized on a sign posted among the vines. The first harvest was in 1983.

"Most everything is hand done," explained John, as he and a friend lovingly applied labels to and polished a case of bottles. Although the Ottemans anticipate an expanded warehouse and a new storage cellar, they plan to keep the winery small.

In addition to their prize-winning Chardonnay, the Ottemans are proud of their distinctive label, the detail work for which was drawn by an engraver from Smith and Wesson, the arms manufacturer. (John is a collector of antique small arms.)

Sarah's, which once opened its gates on weekends for public tastings without appointment, now offers tours and tastings on a call-ahead basis, the result of growing demand for the Ottemans' wines. According to John, "Our wine is virtually all spoken for."

4005 Hecker Pass Road
Gilroy, CA 95020
(408) 842-4278

HOURS: By appointment
TASTINGS: By appointment
TOURS: By appointment
PICNIC AREA: No
RETAIL SALES: Yes
DIRECTIONS: East of Watsonville Road intersection on Hecker Pass Road (Highway 152).
VINTNER'S CHOICE: Chardonnay

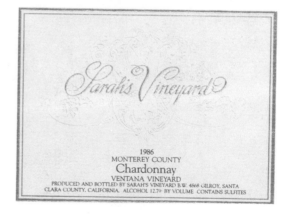

1986
MONTEREY COUNTY
Chardonnay
VENTANA VINEYARD
PRODUCED AND BOTTLED BY SARAH'S VINEYARD B.W. 4868 GILROY, SANTA CLARA COUNTY, CALIFORNIA. ALCOHOL 12.7% BY VOLUME. CONTAINS SULFITES

Summerhill Vineyards

Gilroy

With its contemporary ranch-style tasting room, Summerhill Vineyards presents an image of a newer winery. First impressions can be deceiving, however; this venerable estate has been producing wine since the Bertero family founded the operation in 1917.

Although the Berteros no longer own the property, the winery is still a family business. The husband-wife team of Debra Dodd and Red Johnson left Carmel to operate Summerhill as a small corporation comprising family friends.

Debra and Red prefer not to lead tours through the winemaking facilities, steering visitors instead to one of the more comfortable tasting rooms in the area. In addition to daily tastings, Summerhill offers outdoor Sunday brunches from May through October. The winery also hosts an end-of-harvest dinner that doubles as a Halloween costume party. Details of the special events are included in Summerhill's newsletter.

Among Summerhill's lengthy roster of varietals and generics are several fruit wines and an Italian after-dinner wine called Aleatico, which is produced at only one other California winery.

3920 Hecker Pass Road
Gilroy, CA 95020
(408) 842-3032

HOURS: 9 A.M.–6 P.M. daily
TASTINGS: Yes
TOURS: No
PICNIC AREA: Yes
RETAIL SALES: Yes
DIRECTIONS: Four miles west of Highway 101 in Gilroy on Hecker Pass Road (Highway 152).
VINTNER'S CHOICE: Cabernet Sauvignon Blanc

CLASSIC CALIFORNIA

RIESLING

light in style and fruity, almost dry. Excellent with salad, seafood, or as a social wine. Serve slightly chilled.

CELLARED AND BOTTLED IN THE SHADOWS OF STEINBECK'S BELOVED COASTAL GAVILAN MOUNTAINS BY

SUMMERHILL VINEYARDS

Bonded Winery CA 1625 • Carmel, California • Alcohol 12% by Volume

Live Oaks Winery

Gilroy

After a full day spent with several vintners of the Hecker Pass area, I hesitated before driving down the lane to Peter Scagliotti's Live Oaks Winery. From the road, the nondescript group of old buildings didn't appear to offer anything that I hadn't already seen.

My preconceptions were shattered when I stepped into what has to be one of Northern California's most eccentric tasting rooms. While Peter is a collector, he's not your typical collector. The large room is crammed with groupings of unconventional bric-a-brac. On one wall hang hundreds of business cards and vehicle license plates. Animal trophies are mounted on another. Behind the bar is an assemblage of foreign currency, while Christmas ornaments dangle (this was in May) from the ceiling.

The other buildings at Live Oaks Winery aren't open to the public, but most visitors seem content to browse among the curios that fill the tasting room. Peter does, however, maintain a comfortable picnic area and barbecue just outside the tasting room door.

Live Oaks, which was founded in 1912 by Peter's Italian immigrant father, Eduardo, is known for its premium-quality Burgundy. This blend of vintages and varieties is aged for more than five years before release.

3875 Hecker Pass Road
Gilroy, CA 95020
(408) 842-2401

HOURS: 10 A.M.–5 P.M. daily; closed major holidays
TASTINGS: Yes
TOURS: No
PICNIC AREA: Yes
RETAIL SALES: Yes
DIRECTIONS: Four-and-a-half miles from downtown Gilroy on Hecker Pass Road (Highway 152).
VINTNER'S CHOICE: Burgundy

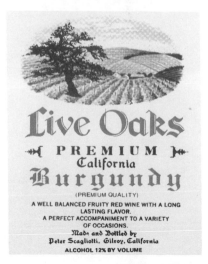

Live Oaks
⊷❴ PREMIUM ❵↢
California
Burgundy
(PREMIUM QUALITY)
A WELL BALANCED FRUITY RED WINE WITH A LONG LASTING FLAVOR.
A PERFECT ACCOMPANIMENT TO A VARIETY OF OCCASIONS.
Made and Bottled by
Peter Scagliotti, Gilroy, California
ALCOHOL 12% BY VOLUME

SOQUEL TO HALF MOON BAY

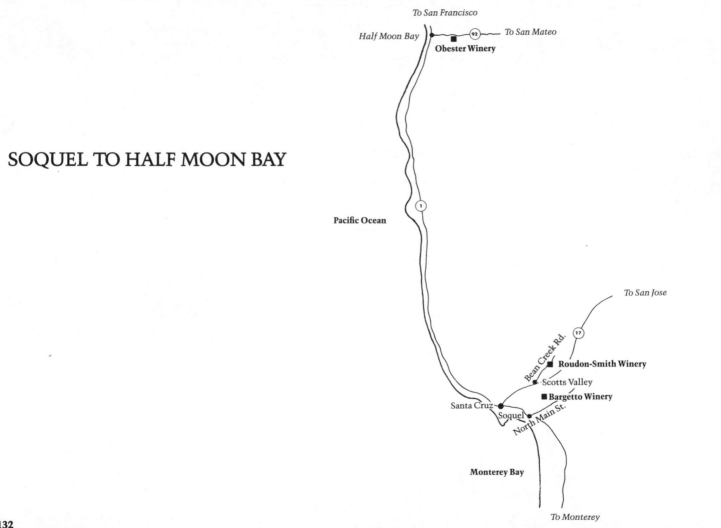

Bargetto Winery
Soquel

At Bargetto Winery in Soquel, winemaking is not *just* a family affair, it's almost exclusively a family affair. Beverly, Martin, John, Richard, Loretta, Donna, Peter, James, and Tom all share the family name; each lends his or her own special talent to the operation.

Bargetto has been a fixture of this Santa Cruz County hamlet since 1933, the year Prohibition ended. John and Philip Bargetto, sons of an Italian winemaker who immigrated in the late 1800s, chose the year of Repeal to convert their truck farm to a small winery. They began, inauspiciously enough, making bulk wines for local retailers and restaurants.

John's son Lawrence guided the operation into its second generation and introduced fruit wines to the Bargetto roster. The apricot, pomegranate, raspberry, and olallieberry wines are still some of Bargetto's most popular.

After Lawrence's death in 1982, his widow, Beverly, assumed the presidency of the company. Son Martin serves as general manager, with a cadre of dedicated siblings and cousins rounding out the list of Bargetto staff.

Using grapes from other California vintners, the Bargetto family produces a number of varietals, including Johannisberg Riesling, Gewürztraminer, Chardonnay, Zinfandel, White Zinfandel, and Cabernet Sauvignon. The winery, housed in a tidy brown barn, also offers patrons a Blanc de Noir *méthode champenoise* and a series of dessert wines imported from Italy.

In comfort and ambience, the Bargetto tasting room has few rivals. The narrow room with full-length bar and rustic panelling perches at the edge of Soquel Creek. The homey environment indoors coupled with the peaceful setting beyond the windows lend themselves to lingering visits. Tastings also are conducted under blue skies in an adjacent garden courtyard.

3535 North Main Street
Soquel, CA 95073
(408) 475-2258

HOURS: 10 A.M.–5:30 P.M. daily; closed major holidays
TASTINGS: Yes
TOURS: 11 A.M.– and 2 P.M. weekdays, by appointment
PICNIC AREA: No
RETAIL SALES: Yes
DIRECTIONS: From Highway 1, take Capitola-Soquel exit north to Main Street, turn right; 1 mile to winery.
VINTNER'S CHOICE: Chardonnay

50th ANNIVERSARY
1933-1983

1981
CALIFORNIA
Chardonnay
SANTA BARBARA COUNTY

Bargetto

PRODUCED AND BOTTLED BY BARGETTO'S SANTA CRUZ WINERY
SOQUEL, CALIFORNIA. ALCOHOL 12.8% BY VOLUME

Roudon-Smith Vineyards

Scotts Valley

2364 Bean Creek Road
Santa Cruz, CA 95066
(408) 438-1244

HOURS: Saturday, by appointment
TASTINGS: Saturday, by appointment
TOURS: Saturday, by appointment
PICNIC AREA: Yes
RETAIL SALES: Yes
DIRECTIONS: Call for appointment and
    directions.
VINTNER'S CHOICE: Zinfandel

It had the makings of a contemporary Northern California success story: The engineering whiz who starts a promising manufacturing operation in high-tech Silicon Valley and gains fame and fortune. Jim Smith's story had most of the ingredients until fate stepped in and he hired Bob Roudon (Roo-DON) to help get the operation going. Bob, as it turned out, had different plans for himself and his new colleague, and it wasn't long before Jim was convinced to leave the Santa Clara Valley rat race and establish a vineyard and winery in the Santa Cruz foothills.

The Roudon and Smith families launched their partnership in 1971 with the planting of a small Chardonnay vineyard and the purchase of eighteen tons of grapes. The basement of Bob and Annamarie Roudon's Santa Cruz Mountains home served as the original winery until Jim and June Smith moved to a rural plot of land on Bean Creek Road and plans were drawn for a new winemaking facility. The two former engineers built much of the modest, fir-sided building themselves and even designed a few one-of-a-kind pieces of equipment for the winery.

In its relatively young life, Roudon-Smith has won praise from major wine critics and amassed a number of prestigious California wine awards. Contributing to the efforts are Annamaria, who handles the finances and designs the labels, and June, who does the winery's public relations and marketing work.

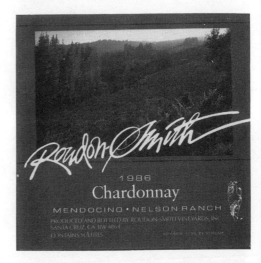

Obester Winery

Half Moon Bay

The late John Gemello, who figured prominently in the post-Repeal rebirth of the Santa Clara Valley wine industry with his own winery, also left a legacy over the mountains in Half Moon Bay, where a young couple is quietly carrying on a tradition begun in Italy nearly a century ago.

"It's strange the way things turn out," said Gemello's granddaughter, Sandy, recalling the events that led her and her husband, Paul Obester, to establish their small winery near the Pacific Ocean.

Several years after retiring from his winemaking business in Mountain View, the elder Gemello went to live with Sandy and Paul. In an attempt to provide her ninety-three-year-old grandfather with a project to occupy his time, Sandy suggested that he teach the family how to make wine. "One thing led to another," said Sandy, and the hobby evolved into a vocation when Paul, a Stanford University–educated Silicon Valley marketing executive, left his job to pursue a second career as winemaker. The Obesters bought some land on the outskirts of Half Moon Bay and established the winery in 1977.

Before John Gemello's death, at the age of ninety-eight, the master winemaker touched another, even younger generation. Paul and Sandy's oldest son, Doug, studied at the University of California, Davis, and as winemaker at both Obester and Gemello has already stepped into his grandfather's shoes.

Obester (the accent is on the *O*) sits in a small valley beside the country highway that connects Half Moon Bay with San Mateo. An aging tin-sided hay barn functions as the production facility. Visitors are welcomed at a spacious and rustic tasting room that the Obesters fashioned from a carport. A picture window frames a scenic view of the valley.

12341 San Mateo Road
Half Moon Bay, CA 94019
(415) 726-9463

HOURS: 10 A.M.–5 P.M. Friday–Sunday;
Noon–5 P.M. Monday–Thursday
TASTINGS: Yes
TOURS: By appointment
PICNIC AREA: Yes
RETAIL SALES: Yes
DIRECTIONS: From Highway 1,
2 miles east on San Mateo Road
(Highway 92).
VINTNER'S CHOICE: Johannisberg Riesling

CARMEL TO TEMPLETON

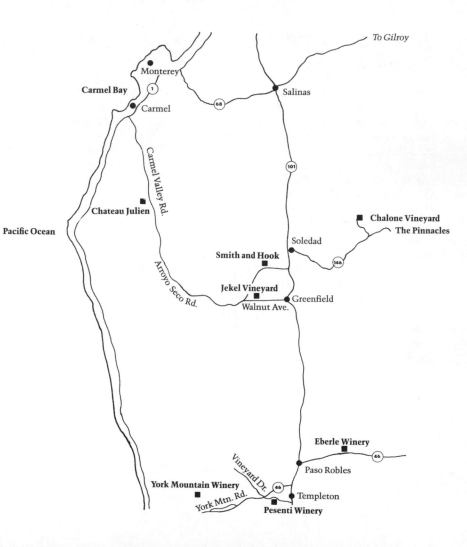

To Gilroy

Monterey

Carmel Bay

1

Carmel

68

Salinas

101

Chateau Julien

Carmel Valley Rd.

Pacific Ocean

■ **Chalone Vineyard**
The Pinnacles

Soledad

146

Smith and Hook

Arroyo Seco Rd.

Jekel Vineyard

Greenfield

Walnut Ave.

Eberle Winery

46

Vineyard Dr.

Paso Robles

York Mountain Winery

46

York Mtn. Rd.

Templeton

Pesenti Winery

Chateau Julien
Carmel

The corporate offices of an East Coast oil company are a long way, both physically and figuratively, from a wine estate on the California coast. Nonetheless, petroleum company executive Bob Brower and his wife, Pat, were happy to trade their existence in New York for life in peaceful Carmel Valley.

As the winery's name and appearance suggest, the Browers were inspired by the fine country wineries of France. Wines are produced in the French claret tradition of Bordeaux, using state-of-the-art equipment and imported bottles. The French oak cooperage is exchanged for new barrels after each vintage.

Chateau Julien has only a small experimental vineyard on site and consequently purchases grapes from growers elsewhere in Monterey County and from the Paso Robles region, farther south. The roster here includes Chardonnay, Sauvignon Blanc, Fumé Blanc, Merlot, and Cabernet Sauvignon. Chateau Julien also produces Julien Dry Sherry, Carmel Cream Sherry, and two table wines.

The chateau itself, which was to be expanded for additional storage, is a grand two-story building of white plaster, built in 1983, one year after the first vintage. In additon to the Great Hall reception and tasting area with its tiled floor and stained glass windows, the building contains offices and an elegant conference room for private functions. Barrels are stored adjacent to the fermentation tanks at the opposite end of the facility, while production equipment is set on a pad outside.

Local ordinances discourage drop-in visits for tours and tastings. "Invitations" are available by calling in advance.

8940 Carmel Valley Road
Carmel, CA 93923
(408) 624-2600

HOURS: 8:30 A.M.–5 P.M. Monday–Friday, Noon–5 P.M. Saturday and Sunday; call for "invitation."
TASTINGS: Yes
TOURS: By appointment
PICNIC AREA: No
RETAIL SALES: Yes
DIRECTIONS: Five miles east of Highway 1 on Carmel Valley Road.
VINTNER'S CHOICE: Chardonnay

Smith and Hook

Gonzales

"A commitment to Cabernet" is the slogan of Smith and Hook, a wine estate whose sole product is—you guessed it. Some 250 rolling acres on the eastern slope of the Santa Lucia Mountains provide the panoramic setting for this interesting looking winery.

The operation is housed in an old barn whose former occupants were quarter horses. The stable sits on the old Smith Ranch, while the adjacent Hook property is planted to grapes—hence the winery's name.

The site, which affords breathtaking views of the Salinas Valley and Gavilan Mountains, was chosen in 1973 by the McFarland Wine Company of Southern California. The McFarlands, longtime wine grape growers, concentrated their planting efforts on Cabernet vines and celebrated their first harvest in 1979.

The family may have drastically altered the function of the old horse ranch, but they preserved the property's rustic look. The stable was reconditioned to house winemaking equipment, open redwood fermentors, and rows of barrels. The old tack room is now the laboratory, and what was a bunkhouse now serves as an office. Guests are welcomed at another original building that overlooks the valley. The only new facility is a warehouse built to accommodate small oak cooperage.

Grapes from the several varying slopes and valleys of the vineyard are hand picked and crushed in separate batches. After one year of aging, the wines are blended (along with some Merlot) to obtain the desired quality. Smith and Hook wines are aged for three years—or even longer, if the winemaker so chooses.

37700 Foothill Road
P.O. Box 1010
Gonzales, CA 93926
(408) 678-2132

HOURS: By appointment
TASTINGS: By appointment
TOURS: By appointment
PICNIC AREA: Yes
RETAIL SALES: No
DIRECTIONS: From Highway 101, west on Arroyo Seco Road, right on Fort Romie, left on Colony, right on Foothill, and left on driveway at school.
VINTNER'S CHOICE: Cabernet Sauvignon (their only wine)

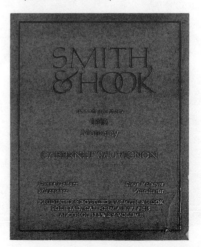

Chalone Vineyard

Soledad

Chalone Vineyard takes its name from an extinct volcano that shaped the Gavilan Range centuries ago. The region's grape-growing potential was tapped in the early 1900s by a Frenchman who discovered conditions that compared favorably with the famous Cote d'Or of his homeland. Vines planted during the 1920s and 1940s first produced grapes that were sent away and used in making Soledad Champagne.

Since then the property has seen a succession of proprietors. Earlier owners constructed a tidy little winery, which now holds Chalone's library of older vintages. Today, the little oak-shaded, whitewashed building is dwarfed by a modern winery, which has a provision for even further expansion should production warrant.

Chalone, which started out in the mid sixties as a small partnership, is now a publicly held company—a rarity nowadays in the California winemaking industry. Chairman of the board Richard Graff, vineyard manager Bob Roche, and winemaker Michael Michaud supervise the hand picking of berries in small lots, with each acre yielding only about three to five barrels of wine.

While much of Chalone's acreage of vineyard is relatively new, the original vines still produce. In fact, the reserve wines from these craggy old vines are available only to mailing list customers and to those who write for an appointment and make the half-hour trek from the valley floor up to this oldest winery in Monterey County.

Stonewall Canyon Road
P.O. Box 855
Soledad, CA 93960
(415) 546-7755 or (408) 678-1717

HOURS: By appointment (please write for appointment)
TASTINGS: By appointment, or Saturday, 10 A.M.–3:30 P.M.
TOURS: By appointment
PICNIC AREA: No
RETAIL SALES: Yes
DIRECTIONS: From Soledad, 9 miles east on Highway 146; 1 mile on Stonewall Canyon Road to winery.
VINTNER'S CHOICES: Chardonnay and Pinot Noir

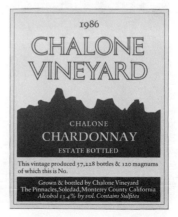

1986
CHALONE VINEYARD

CHALONE
CHARDONNAY
ESTATE BOTTLED

This vintage produced 57,228 bottles & 120 magnums of which this is No.

Grown & bottled by Chalone Vineyard
The Pinnacles, Soledad, Monterey County California
Alcohol 13.4% by vol. Contains Sulfites

Jekel Vineyard
Greenfield

From a distance, Jekel Vineyard more closely resembles a rambling country estate. In addition to a weathered old barn, there's a windmill and a new red, two-story addition that from the road looks like a fine old ranch house.

A winery it is, however, albeit a new one. The Jekel family established their vineyard on the outskirts of Greenfield in 1972, converting row crops to vines. The winery followed six years later. When I visited Jekel, more than 300 acres were under cultivation, providing the winery with enough grapes to produce 80,000 cases per year.

Production is centered in a large galvanized barn painted red. Towering stainless steel fermentors, a laboratory, barrel storage, and a bottling room are within a few steps of each other. While a tour of Jekel's facilities is worthwhile, visitors can also view some of the operation from interior windows in the intimate tasting room.

With the completion of a new wing, the Jekel family transferred the business headquarters from their home base in Southern California to the winery. Along with the offices, the addition houses a hospitality area that accommodates group luncheons and tastings.

The lengthy and cool growing season of the Arroyo Seco region enables Jekel to produce some award-winning wines, including Johannisberg Riesling, Chardonnay, Pinot Blanc, Pinot Noir, and Cabernet Sauvignon.

40155 Walnut Avenue
Greenfield, CA 93927
(408) 674-5522

HOURS: 10 A.M.–5 P.M. daily
TASTINGS: Yes
TOURS: By appointment
PICNIC AREA: Yes
RETAIL SALES: Yes
DIRECTIONS: One mile west of Highway 101 on Walnut Avenue.
VINTNER'S CHOICE: Johannisberg Riesling

Eberle Winery

Paso Robles

Eberle Winery had been open scarcely one week when I first happened by, a few years ago. Gary and Jeanie Eberle were still applying the finishing touches to the sparkling wood-sided facility that perches on a hill a few miles east of Paso Robles.

The Eberles' first priority was building the winery, and in doing so, the couple went first class. The tasting room is a large one, trimmed with oak and sporting a large, tiled fireplace. From one window, visitors can view the outdoor crushing pad; from another, the interior fermentation and storage areas can be seen. At the end of the bar, French doors open to a covered patio that overlooks the expansive estate and the hills beyond.

Prior to establishing his own winery, Gary, who played football at Penn State under Joe Paterno, practiced the vintner's art at nearby Estrella Winery, which he designed and built. Also a wine industry veteran, Jeanie operates a wine wholesale business.

Gary's 1980 Cabernet accompanied President Reagan on his 1984 trip to China. This vintage was part of the seventy-fifth anniversary memento wine collection of the University of California, Davis.

The Eberle roster, described by the proprietors as "short and serious," focuses on Cabernet Sauvignon and Chardonnay, with some Muscat Canelli and a Sauvignon Blanc thrown in for good measure.

Highway 46
P.O. Box 2459
Paso Robles, CA 93447
(805) 238-9607

HOURS: 10A.M.–5 P.M. daily; closed major holidays
TASTINGS: Yes
TOURS: Yes
PICNIC AREA: Yes
RETAIL SALES: Yes
DIRECTIONS: Four miles east of Highway 101 on Highway 46.
VINTNER'S CHOICE: Cabernet Sauvignon

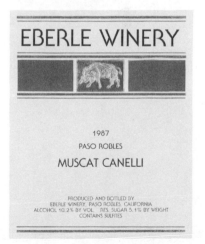

EBERLE WINERY

1987
PASO ROBLES
MUSCAT CANELLI

PRODUCED AND BOTTLED BY
EBERLE WINERY, PASO ROBLES, CALIFORNIA
ALCOHOL 10.2% BY VOL. RES. SUGAR 5.1% BY WEIGHT
CONTAINS SULFITES

Pesenti Winery

Templeton

For a relatively small, family-run business, Pesenti Winery offers an unusually lengthy list of wines. The more than eighty different types are not a roster for the indecisive wine enthusiast.

Some of the wines are made from grapes that flourish among original vines planted by founders Frank and Caterina Pesenti in 1923. A native of Bergamo, Italy, Frank had to wait until Prohibition ended to establish his winery. The original, built in 1934, has since been enlarged twice, as business grew.

The facility consists of two large, plain buildings painted white. One contains concrete fermentation tanks, crushing equipment, and the tasting room, where the array of Pesenti wines covers almost every inch of wall space. Aging and bottling take place in the adjacent masonry building. The family homestead stands nearby.

Frank's son, Vic, son-in-law, Al Nerelli, and Al's son, Frank, share the operation of the winery these days. While poking around the place, I asked a winery employee for the name of Pesenti's winemaker. "We all help make wine," he joked. "Everybody gets to work their feet."

2900 Vineyard Drive
Templeton, CA 93465
(805) 434-1030

HOURS: 8 A.M.–5:30 P.M. Monday– Saturday; 9 A.M.–5:30 P.M. Sunday
TASTINGS: Yes
TOURS: Given informally
PICNIC AREA: No
RETAIL SALES: Yes
DIRECTIONS: From Highway 101 south of Paso Robles, take Vineyard Drive exit, west 2.5 miles to winery.
VINTNER'S CHOICE: Zinfandel

York Mountain Winery

Templeton

York Mountain Winery has written its share of Templeton region wine-making history. This venerable establishment celebrated its centennial in 1982, making it one of the Central Coast's oldest wineries.

The establishment was christened Ascension Winery by Andrew York, who grew grapes and made small amounts of wine here in the late 1800s. The winery remained in the York family until Max Goldman purchased it in 1970. Max's son Steve is the winemaker; daughter Suzanne works the tasting room and gift area.

The Goldmans' operation is as rustic as you'll find in these parts. The brick-walled, dimly lit tasting room has a wood floor, a rustic stone fireplace, and an assortment of antique bric-a-brac. Outside is a small deck with a bench facing the scenic hills and vines.

Although Max bought the property with plans to concentrate on Champagne, other wines have crept onto the roster. York Mountain produces Zinfandel, Chardonnay, Merlot, Pinot Noir, Cabernet Sauvignon, two types of Champagne, Red and White wines, Rosé, Claret, Dry Sherry, and Port.

York Mountain Road
Route 2, Box 191
Templeton, CA 93465
(805) 238-3925

HOURS: 10 A.M.–5 P.M. daily
TASTINGS: Yes
TOURS: By appointment
PICNIC AREA: No
RETAIL SALES: Yes
DIRECTIONS: From Highway 101 south of Paso Robles, take Highway 46 west for 9 miles; north at first or second York Mountain Road sign.
VINTNER'S CHOICE: Zinfandel

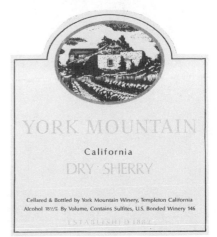

YORK MOUNTAIN

California

DRY SHERRY

Cellared & Bottled by York Mountain Winery, Templeton California
Alcohol 18½% By Volume, Contains Sulfites, U.S. Bonded Winery 146

ESTABLISHED 1882

THE MOTHER LODE AND CENTRAL VALLEY

There's Grapes in Them Thar Hills

California's Mother Lode is in the midst of a boom the likes of which hasn't been seen since James Marshall touched off the Gold Rush in 1848. Today's attraction is the grape. A prominent wine-producing region during the last part of the nineteenth century and early part of the twentieth, the Sierra foothills later lost hundreds of acres of vineyards to phylloxera and through neglect during the years of Prohibition.

The gold country is rapidly making up for lost time; I found new vineyards emerging on hillsides and in valleys from Nevada County to Calaveras County. Wineries have likewise been springing up in recent years—so fast, in fact, that it's difficult to maintain a current count. While winemaking operations are scattered about much of the countryside, the highest concentrations are to be found east of Highway 49 along the northern portion of Amador County, which is near Plymouth, and in El Dorado County, between Fairplay and Apple Hill.

The scenic back roads and tranquil towns—not to mention friendly vintners—make it difficult to leave this region after just one day. Consequently, if you're planning an overnight stay, consider the Mother Lode's array of historic small hotels and inns. Among the quaint hostelries along your tour besides those recommended below are the Hotel Leger in Mokelumne Hill, the Sutter Creek Inn in Sutter Creek, and the National Hotel in Nevada City.

During the harvest season, when tourist attention is heaped upon the Napa and Sonoma grape-growing regions, the back roads of the Mother Lode present a delightful and relatively uncrowded alternative for wine enthusiasts and California adventurers.

The Amador County Chamber of Commerce publishes a visitors' guide (see the Wine Tour Maps section at the back of this book) that lists its member wineries as well as other helpful information for those planning a trip into the hills.

The industry may be undergoing a rebirth in the foothills, but winemaking has flourished for years in the San Joaquin Valley. Considering the vastness of this wine-producing region and its tremendous contribution of grapes to the state's wine industry, one would think tasting rooms would be plentiful. Actually, they are few, and even farther between.

I found myself attracted to the dwindling number of informal family-operated wineries that have been longtime valley fixtures. A visit with the Nonini family at their Fresno winery, for example, was among the highlights of my travels through Northern California's wine country. Winemaker Reno Nonini greets his guests at a tiny, unpretentious room where they sip valley vintages not in crystal glasses but from paper cups, pulled from a wall dispenser. This is backroad wining at its most engaging.

Spending the night?

The Murphys Hotel, a refurbished, Gold Rush–era hotel that's hosted the likes of Gen. Ulysses Grant. His bed is still here. 457 Main Street, Murphys, CA 95247; (209) 728-3454.

The Jamestown Hotel, another mining days relic, which has been completely reconstructed and furnished with comfy antiques. Main Street (P.O. Box 539), Jamestown, CA 95327; (209) 984-3904.

MURPHYS TO APPLE HILL

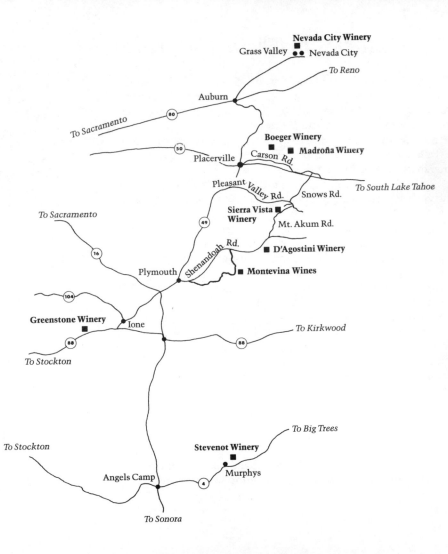

Murphys to Apple Hill
(Including Nevada City)

Stevenot Winery

Murphys

For many years Mercer Cavern provided the only reason for tourists to venture down Sheep Ranch Road out of the little town of Murphys. Since Barden Stevenot established a vineyard in the neighborhood in 1976, however, the cavern has learned to share the spotlight.

The winery that bears Stevenot's name sits a couple of miles from Murphys in a small canyon ringed by oak and pine. Old-timers might remember the spread as the Shaw Ranch, site of Calaveras County's first swimming pool.

The homestead and pool are still here, but the cattle have been replaced by nearly thirty acres of young vines. The age of the winery notwithstanding, Stevenot (the second *t* is silent) boasts a lengthy list of regional and state awards. Stevenot also produces Chardonnay, Chenin Blanc, Cabernet Sauvignon, and a Zinfandel that is served at Yosemite's famed Ahwahnee Hotel.

A number of renovated ranch buildings compose the operation. Stevenot, whose family has resided in the county for five generations, lives in the stately old home. A barn that dates back to the 1890s houses the winemaking equipment. When things occasionally go awry here, workers blame the ghost of an Indian who, according to legend, was hanged in the barn long ago.

Of similar vintage is Stevenot's one-of-a-kind tasting room. Alaska House, as it is known, is an old log-walled, sod-roofed cellar of sorts, cut into a gentle grassy slope near the house. Rancher Shaw, who settled the property, chose this architectural style after returning from journeys to the Alaskan wilderness, where such earth-covered structures were common. At one time, this rustic bower, built in 1908, was home to a convicted murderer whom Shaw befriended.

But like the proverbial wine that mellows with age, the wild activities that colored the early years of the ranch have given way to a more respectable standing for Stevenot as one of the gold country's preeminent wineries.

2690 San Domingo Road
P.O. Box 548
Murphys, CA 95247
(209) 728-3436

HOURS: 10 A.M.–5 P.M. daily; closed major holidays
TASTINGS: Yes
TOURS: Weekdays only
PICNIC AREA: Yes
RETAIL SALES: Yes
DIRECTIONS: At Murphys Hotel, take Sheep Ranch Road/San Domingo Road for 2.5 miles; winery is 1 mile past Mercer Cavern.
VINTNER'S CHOICE: Cabernet Sauvignon

Calaveras County
CHENIN BLANC
1987

Stevenot

PRODUCED AND BOTTLED BY
STEVENOT WINERY B.W. 4839
MURPHYS, CALAVERAS COUNTY, CALIFORNIA
ALCOHOL 12.5% BY VOLUME CONTAINS SULFITES

Greenstone Winery

Ione

A nationwide search for just the right spot brought two young Southern California families to the base of the Amador County foothills near Ione. Home winemakers Stan and Karen Van Spanje and Durward and Jane Fowler claimed the site in 1980 after touring the United States looking for a vineyard and winery location.

Situated a quarter of a mile off Highway 88, Greenstone started out as a part-time project for the couples, who divided their time between teaching jobs in Southern California and their vineyard in the Sierra foothills. Then, in 1983 Stan and Durward left the classroom to devote their full attention to the growing winemaking operation. Because Karen and Jane still teach in neighboring Sutter Creek and Jackson, the winery observes an adapted school schedule: open for visitors on Fridays and weekends only during the academic year and Wednesday through Sunday during much of the summer.

The vines at Greenstone were planted in rich soil around rock outcroppings. For the winery, the owners chose a peaceful spot amongst gnarled oaks at the foot of the hills. Gables and a steep roof adorn the picturesque building, fashioned in the style of a French country barn.

The crusher and press are located outside, leaving the barn for storage. Stan even uses the ample air space inside by baking his sherry on the fourth floor, forty feet above terra firma.

In addition to its own twenty-plus acres of grapes, Greenstone uses grapes from other Amador County vineyards to produce some 8,500 cases of more than a half-dozen different wines. Topping the roster are a White Zinfandel and a Colombard that sell as fast as the vintners can bottle them.

P.O. Box 1164
Ione, CA 95640
(209) 274-2238

HOURS: 10 A.M.–4 P.M. Friday–Sunday; same hours Wednesday–Sunday in July and August
TASTINGS: Yes
TOURS: Given informally
PICNIC AREA: Yes
RETAIL SALES: Yes
DIRECTIONS: At Highway 88 and Jackson Valley Road, southwest of Ione.
VINTNER'S CHOICE: Zinfandel Port

D'Agostini Winery
Plymouth

The Shenandoah Valley east of Plymouth has in recent years become a home to nearly a dozen small winemaking operations. However, even the combination of their years of operation can't come close to matching the more than a century of winemaking at D'Agostini, patriarch of Mother Lode wineries.

A state historical landmark, D'Agostini was established by Adam Uhlinger, who began planting vines here as early as 1856, when the local population was given more to tearing up the hills than to cultivating them.

Enrico D'Agostini, an Italian immigrant, acquired the operation from Uhlinger's son in 1911, signaling the start of another two generations of family operation. Brothers Henry, Michele, Tulio, and Armenio inherited the winery when their father died in the mid fifties. With the siblings approaching retirement age and their children choosing other vocations, the D'Agostinis sold the winery in 1984.

The first stop for visitors is usually an informal tasting room, housed in the concrete block building nearest the road. The real treat, however, is a self-guided walk through the labyrinthine cellar of locally quarried stone. Here oval oak barrels, some as old as the winery itself, share space with 17,000-gallon casks that tower over visitors. The making of D'Agostini wines takes place in an adjacent covered area. The grand old homestead sits atop the cellar.

Despite the impression created by the hulking cellar casks, D'Agostini is a small winery by industry standards, with attention to quality receiving a higher priority than quantity.

Route 2, Box 19
Plymouth, CA 95669
(209) 245-6612

HOURS: 9 A.M.–4:30 P.M. daily; closed major holidays
TASTINGS: Yes
TOURS: Given informally
PICNIC AREA: No
RETAIL SALES: Yes
DIRECTIONS: Eight miles northeast of Plymouth on Shenandoah Road
VINTNER'S CHOICE: Zinfandel

Estate Bottled

D'Agostini

WINERY
EST. 1856

CALIFORNIA
ZINFANDEL
ALCOHOL 13% BY VOLUME

PRODUCED AND BOTTLED BY
D'AGOSTINI WINERY • PLYMOUTH, AMADOR CO., CALIF.

Monteviña Wines
Plymouth

Unlike many retirees from the big cities who drift up to California's gold country to swing in a hammock, Walter Field started a new career with Monteviña Wines.

A pioneer of sorts (Monteviña's first release was in 1973), Field deserves much of the credit for helping to lead the Mother Lode winemaking renaissance of the 1970s.

In staking out his foothill claim for Monteviña, Field chose a remote spot. If you thought the hamlet of Plymouth was off the beaten track, just wait. The winery is another five miles beyond, virtually hidden among the proliferating vineyards of the beautiful Shenandoah Valley. (The extra miles are worth the effort, however.)

The second chapter in Monteviña's story began in 1988 when Field sold the property to Napa Valley-based Sutter Home Winery.

After a sip or two inside the cool tasting room, we selected a bottle of Monteviña wine and adjourned to a quiet table in the shaded picnic area to savor the lush environs.

The selection up here includes the Mother Lode–requisite Zinfandel as well as Fumé Blanc, White Zinfandel, Barbera, Chardonnay, and Cabernet Sauvignon.

20680 Shenandoah School Road
Plymouth, CA 95669
(209) 245-6942

HOURS: 11 A.M.–4 P.M. daily
TASTINGS: Yes
TOURS: No
PICNIC AREA: Yes
RETAIL SALES: Yes
DIRECTIONS: From Highway 16/49 in Plymouth, east on Shenandoah Road for 2.5 miles, right on Shenandoah School Road for 2 miles to winery.
VINTNER'S CHOICE: Zinfandel

1985
Monteviña™
SHENANDOAH VALLEY
CALIFORNIA
ZINFANDEL MONTINO
ESTATE BOTTLED
GROWN, PRODUCED & BOTTLED BY MONTEVIÑA WINES, AMADOR COUNTY, PLYMOUTH, CA
ALC. 12.5% BY VOL. CONTAINS SULFITES

Sierra Vista Winery

Placerville

The decision to establish a vineyard in the Sierra foothills signaled a radical change for John MacCready and his family. In leaving their native Ohio in 1973, John traded a comfortable career in electrical engineering, in which he holds a Ph.D., for the relatively insecure life of a farmer.

The family chose to sink new roots near the sleepy hamlet of Pleasant Valley. John faced a formidable task in establishing his vineyard in 1977, laboring long and hard clearing trees and brush. He was rewarded not only with a healthy thirty-one-acre plot of vines but with a breathtaking Sierra view long obscured by trees. The native ponderosa pines removed in the process provided the wood for John's rustic winery, which sits near the family home.

John and his wife, Barbara, who have joined the legion of winemakers rediscovering the grape-growing potential of the Mother Lode, produce about 7,500 cases each year. They invite visitors to drop by the winery for a weekend taste of Sierra Vista's Cabernet Sauvignon, Fumé Blanc, White and Red Zinfandel, and Chardonnay. Sierra Sirah from a small test plot is sold only at the winery.

4560 Cabernet Way
Placerville, CA 95667
(916) 622-7221

HOURS: 11 A.M.–5 P.M. Saturday and
Sunday; other times by appointment
TASTINGS: Yes
TOURS: Yes
PICNIC AREA: Yes
RETAIL SALES: Yes
DIRECTIONS: Take Newtowne Road exit
from Highway 50 east of Placerville;
south on Newtowne Road, left on
Pleasant Valley Road, and right on
Leisure Lane to Cabernet Way.
VINTNER'S CHOICE: Cabernet Sauvignon

Sierra Vista
ESTATE BOTTLED
1985 EL DORADO
ZINFANDEL
REEVES VINEYARD
Special Reserve
GROWN, PRODUCED & BOTTLED
BY SIERRA VISTA WINERY
PLACERVILLE, CALIFORNIA
CONTAINS SULFITES
ALC. 13.6%
BY VOL.

Madroña

Madroña Vineyards

Camino

With Sierra peaks rising beyond well-kept rows of grapevines, the setting of Madroña Vineyards must rank as one of the most dramatic among California wineries. In terms of elevation—3,000 feet—you won't find a loftier vineyard, at least not in this state.

Dick Bush is the owner of California's highest vineyard, the name of which was inspired by a handsome madrone tree that serves as a centerpiece among the vines. The former engineer and his wife, Leslie, a teacher, planted a thirty-five-acre parcel between 1972 and 1974, but it wasn't until 1980 that ground was broken for the winery. Another four years elapsed before the rustic tasting room was finished.

The winery, a modern, nondescript facility, is situated among conifer and oak trees and is somewhat difficult to locate. Visitors must first pass through either an apple ranch or a Christmas tree farm in order to reach Madroña.

Notwithstanding its location off the beaten path, the winery bustles with activity. I waited in line as the winemaker cheerfully juggled Sunday customers, deliveries, and phone calls.

He does manage to find time to produce 9,000 cases of Madroña Chardonnay, Johannisberg Riesling, Gewürztraminer, White and Red Zinfandel, Cabernet Sauvignon, Merlot, Cabernet Franc, and a dessert wine called Select Harvest Riesling. Dick also serves a separate clientele through custom processing of wines for other operations.

P.O. Box 454
Camino, CA 95709
(916) 644-5948

HOURS: 11 A.M.–5 P.M. Saturday; noon–5 P.M. Sunday
TASTINGS: By appointment
TOURS: By appointment
PICNIC AREA: Informal (no tables)
RETAIL SALES: Yes
DIRECTIONS: From Highway 50 east of Placerville, west on Carson Road, north through High Hill Ranch (apples) to winery.
VINTNER'S CHOICE: Chardonnay and Cabernet Sauvignon

Boeger Winery
Placerville

I discovered Boeger Winery quite by accident several years ago during the fall Apple Hill Days celebration sponsored by local apple growers. Greg and Susan Boeger had only recently set up shop in a new concrete block facility on a hill overlooking the tiny, 1850s Lombardo Winery, now the Boeger tasting room.

The ensuing years have been good to Boeger Winery. Since 1973, its wine has been hailed by critics throughout the nation, won awards too numerous to mention, and even been selected as a presidential gift for a monarch. On a recent return visit, I was delighted to find that success had not spoiled Boeger, which remains one of the gold country's more hospitable and intriguing wineries.

Although dwarfed by the main winery upslope, the tasting room is still Boeger's most prominent building. One of the state's earliest wineries, the diminutive stone and mortar cellar is maintained in a state of arrested decay. Still visible here are the ceiling chutes through which the crushed grapes were once fed from what used to be the production area on the second floor. The old press is displayed along with other memorabilia assembled by the Boegers.

Boeger's annual production of 10,000 cases consists of Chenin Blanc, Chardonnay, Sauvignon Blanc, Zinfandel, Cabernet Sauvignon, and Merlot. The winery bottles blended wines under the popular labels Sierra Blanc, Hangtown Gold, and Hangtown Red. (Placerville was known as Hangtown during the Gold Rush.)

A 1980 Boeger Zinfandel, whose commemorative label bore the inscription "Elizabeth II, Majestic Release, California Zinfandel," was the one presented by President Reagan to Queen Elizabeth during the monarch's 1983 visit to California. The Boeger selection was part of a large gift of California wines judged by the White House as "fit for a queen."

1709 Carson Road
Placerville, CA 95667
(916) 622-8094

HOURS: 10 A.M.–5 P.M. Wednesday–Sunday
TASTINGS: Yes
TOURS: Given informally
PICNIC AREA: Yes
RETAIL SALES: Yes
DIRECTIONS: From Hghway 50 east of Placerville, take the Schnell School Road exit to Carson Road, east to winery drive.
VINTNER'S CHOICE: Merlot

El Dorado
MERLOT
Estate Bottled
1981
PRODUCED AND BOTTLED BY
BOEGER WINERY INC
PLACERVILLE, CALIFORNIA
ALCOHOL 13.3% BY VOLUME

Nevada City Winery
Nevada City

Nevada County's once-thriving winemaking industry, which came to an abrupt halt with Prohibition, seemed destined to become a lost art until a group of wine and grape-growing enthusiasts resurrected the Nevada City Winery in 1980. The 200-or-so acres of grapes now under cultivation in the county pale in comparison to the half-million vines that flourished in the region during the mid-to-late 1800s. Nevertheless, to the owners of Nevada County's only bonded winery, it's a start.

In reestablishing the winery, which a century ago stood a couple of blocks away from the current site, the owners set up shop in a rustic, century-old garage that was part of a foundry next door. (The historic foundry now houses the American Victorian Museum.) Although the garage-turned-winery provides an environment befitting winemaking, the building is nondescript. (In fact, I chose a photo of a more interesting, historic Nevada City scene to illustrate this entry.)

Conversion of the old garage to a small winery involved construction of a mezzanine tasting and sales room, from which visitors can survey the operation and wine production. The upstairs is reserved for barrel aging.

Nevada City Winery stresses production of wines from high elevation grapes, believing that the temperature variance from day to night at the loftier elevations stimulates more character in the flavor of the wine.

321 Spring Street
Nevada City, CA 95959
(916) 265-WINE

HOURS: Noon–5 P.M. daily
TASTINGS: Yes
TOURS: Given informally
PICNIC AREA: No
RETAIL SALES: Yes
DIRECTIONS: "Downtown" in historic Nevada City.
VINTNER'S CHOICE: Douce Noir

FRESNO TO WINTERS

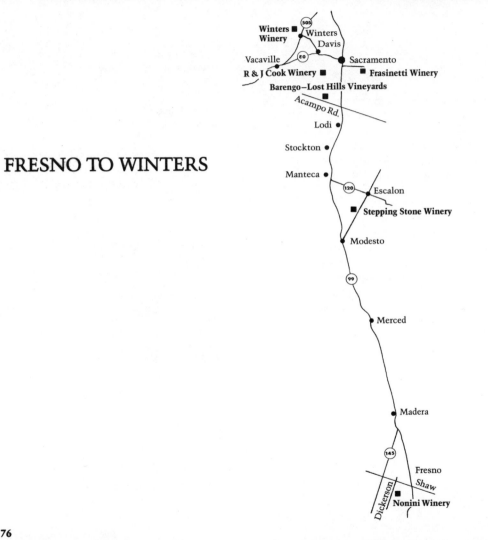

A. Nonini Winery

Fresno

Don't let the urban sprawl of Fresno or the orchards along Highway 99 fool you. This is wine country. According to the Wine Institute, nearly half of California's annual wine grape crop is grown in the rich, warm region around Fresno.

The area is known primarily for the large wineries like Gallo that call this region home. However, serveral small operations are scattered along the back roads. Vineyards are everywhere. Even little Central High School has its own vineyard.

Among the grape-growers who settled the valley in the early twentieth century was Antonio Nonini. An orphan who grew up in the Lombardia area at the base of the Italian Alps, Nonini left his homeland in 1900 at the age of twenty-one to seek a better life in the United States. He bought several acres of western Fresno County land and, with some gentle urging from his son, Reno, established the A. Nonini Winery in 1936.

Reno and his brothers, Geno and Gildo, took over the vineyards and winery after their father's death in 1959. Reno's son Thomas has also taken an active role, as the winery enters its third generation of family operation.

Among Fresno County wineries, A. Nonini is the only one that grows its own product entirely. The Noninis produce table wines, most of which are sold locally. The premium vintages are aged in oak; the others, in redwood tanks.

Tastings are conducted in a one-room cottage tucked between the Nonini homestead and the winery. A paper cup dispenser on the wall gives tasters an indication of the informality of the place. Although the winery is short on pomp, it's long on a hospitable atmosphere that has been a Nonini family tradition for nearly half a century.

2640 North Dickenson Avenue
Fresno, CA 93722
(209) 275-1936

HOURS: 9 A.M.–6 P.M. Monday–Saturday
TASTINGS: Yes
TOURS: Yes
PICNIC AREA: No
RETAIL SALES: Yes
DIRECTIONS: From Highway 99 south, exit at Shaw; west to Dickenson, and south 2.5 miles to winery.
VINTNER'S CHOICES: Zinfandel and Barbera

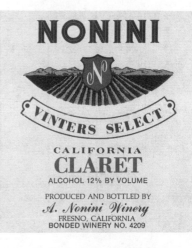

Stepping Stone Vineyards

Escalon

In revising and expanding this book, I discovered that some wineries in the first volume had closed, many had grown, and others had added wines to their rosters. This is the only one that had changed its name. Known for decades as Cadlolo Winery, the facility recently changed hands, and the new owners brought a new name: Stepping Stone Vineyards.

A longtime fixture in tiny Escalon, the winery was established by a Swiss vintner named Louis Sciaroni. Back in 1913, Sciaroni erected foot-thick brick walls to protect his wines from the blazing valley summer heat. The exterior is covered with a lime and sand mortar painted a light pastel.

Cadlolo was the name of Sciaroni's nephew, who purchased the winery in 1937. Cadlolo family members owned the business for many years. The newest owners are the Bavaro Brothers farming company.

Stepping Stone appears quite small from the outside but has a surprising capacity: nearly a quarter of a million gallons. The crusher and fermentation tanks sit outside, next to the railroad tracks.

The only portion of the building not claimed for storage has been turned into a rustic tasting room filled with antiques.

1124 California Street
Escalon, CA 95320
(209) 838-3547

HOURS: Not established at press time; call for hours
TASTINGS: Yes
TOURS: Yes
PICNIC AREA: Yes
RETAIL SALES: Yes
DIRECTIONS: From Highway 120 in Escalon, south on McHenry, right on California Street.
VINTNER'S CHOICE: Mellow Red

Stepping Stone Vineyards

1 · 9 · 8 · 8
CALIFORNIA
CABERNET

PRODUCED & BOTTLED BY STEPPING STONE VINEYARDS
LODI, CALIFORNIA 95240, U.S.A. • ALCOHOL 12% BY VOLUME

Barengo–Lost Hills Vineyards

Acampo

Spindly old palms line the stretch of road from Highway 99 to the tiny Central Valley burg of Acampo, home of Barengo–Lost Hills Vineyards. A valley fixture known for decades simply as Barengo Winery, the business was established in the 1930s by Camillo and Natale Barengo and Cesare Mondavi, father of well-known vintners Robert and Peter Mondavi. Camillo's son Dino later took over the winery.

In revitalizing a facility and equipment that were showing their age, an investment group spent nearly one million dollars, replacing old cooperage with stainless steel, adding a new filtration system, and installing a modern bottling line capable of processing a half-million cases each year. These efforts have resulted in an impressive roster of wine products, including several traditional varietals, German-style May and spiced wines, dessert wines, and wine vinegar. Wines are produced under the Lost Hills and Barengo labels.

While modern technology has caught up with the production areas, the winery has retained its vintage red brick facade. Inside, the tasting room features a handsome copper-covered bar and a selection of deli and gift items. Part of an old 15,000-gallon redwood tank is visible through a large interior window.

3125 East Orange Street
Acampo, CA 95220
(209) 369-2746

HOURS: 9 A.M.–5 P.M. daily
TASTINGS: Yes
TOURS: Yes, by appointment
PICNIC AREA: Yes
RETAIL SALES: Yes
DIRECTIONS: From Highway 99, exit at Acampo Road and drive 1 mile west to winery.
VINTNER'S CHOICES: Barengo Cremapri, Lost Hills White Zinfandel

Lost Hills
VINEYARDS
CALIFORNIA

burgundy
vin-rosé
chablis

Like the vines surrounding the winery, our vineyards have their roots deep in the tradition and history of one of California's most famous wine regions. Our wines are made and bottled in a century old red brick building in the heart of the Sacramento River Delta District. Enjoy for yourself the care and quality we put into each bottle of our award-winning wines.

Frasinetti Winery

Florin (Sacramento)

My first encounter with Frasinetti was as a hungry lunch patron lured off Highway 99 by tales of fine feasting. It wasn't until I approached the property that I realized making food was a relatvely new emphasis. The Frasinettis have been concocting wines much longer than they've been serving pasta.

One of the Sacramento Valley's hidden rural treasures, Frasinetti Winery is tucked away at the edge of a forgotten little suburb originally called Florin, a few miles off Highway 99.

Italian immigrant James Frasinetti built his family winery on this rustic spot back in the 1890s, delivering his wine for many years to Sacramento customers by horse-drawn wagon. In its glory days, Frasinetti boasted 400 acres and was shipping wine by rail to the East Coast.

The ensuing years, however, brought decline to the local agricultural industry and consequent population exodus from Florin.

Today, grandsons Gary and Howard Frasinetti have cut back to the winery's original five acres, combining family tradition and modern technology in making Frasinetti varietals, table wines, dessert wines, fruit wines, and wine vinegar.

The former east cellar has been converted to the rustic restaurant where guests dine within what used to be hulking concrete aging tanks. Other winery bric-a-brac, including old cooperage and vintage equipment, surrounds Frasinetti restaurant guests. A dimly lit, well-stocked tasting room and gift shop sits next to the restaurant and winery.

7395 Frasinetti Road
Sacramento, CA 95828
(916) 383-2444

HOURS: 9 A.M.–9 P.M. Tuesday–Friday;
    11 A.M.–9 P.M. Saturday; 11 A.M.–4 P.M.
    Sunday
TASTINGS: Yes
TOURS: No
PICNIC AREA: No
RETAIL SALES: Yes
DIRECTIONS: From Highway 99 south of
    Sacramento, east on Florin Road for 3
    miles to Frasinetti Road, right to
    winery.
AUTHOR'S CHOICE: White Cabernet

R & J Cook

Clarksburg

If the label depicting an old stern-wheeler suggests that R & J Cook is a bit unusual, a visit to the winery will confirm it. The husband-wife operation is one of very few wineries situated near the banks of the Sacramento River, which once carried riverboat travellers back and forth between the capital city and the Bay Area.

This region, although long famous for its rich soil, has only recently gained any kind of notoriety for grape growing. It was the Cook family that put the Delta on the California winery maps.

The vineyards at Cook date from the late 1960s, when Perry Cook converted a small plot of his row crops to grapes. The quality of the resulting vintage led Perry and son Roger to plant additional vines. Planting expanded in the mid 1970s when Roger established another vineyard nearby in Solano County. Five years later, he and his wife, Joanne, launched their winery with help from their sons.

A tasting room is located next to the winery, which contains an assortment of modern winemaking equipment. The Cooks reside in an adjacent ranch house. The best views of R & J Cook are available from a river levee next to the vines, where Roger and Joanne have built a picnic area for their visitors.

Netherlands Road
P.O. Box 227
Clarksburg, CA 95612
(916) 775-1234

HOURS: 10:30 A.M.–4:30 P.M. weekdays; noon–5 P.M. weekends
TASTINGS: Yes
TOURS: By appointment
PICNIC AREA: Yes
RETAIL SALES: Yes
DIRECTIONS: Drive south from Sacramento for 12 miles along River Road; west on Netherlands Road for 3 miles to winery.
VINTNER'S CHOICE: White Merlot

TABLE WINE
DELTA RED
67% CABERNET SAUVIGNON
22% PETITE SIRAH
11% MERLOT
GROWN, PRODUCED & BOTTLED BY
R. & J. COOK, CLARKSBURG, CA
ALCOHOL 12.5% BY VOLUME
B.W. 4888 CONTAINS SULFITES

Winters Winery

Winters

Winters Winery is the latest occupant of a downtown Winters landmark that since 1876 has housed a general store, butcher shop, bakery, and a turn-of-the-century opera house and dining room.

In contrast to the previous tenants, winemaker David Storm was attracted by the building's thick brick walls and underground cellar, which he found to be well suited for winemaking.

Storm founded Winters Winery here in 1980 after working as a consulting civil and sanitary engineer. In addition to serving as a consultant to wineries on water and wastewater problems, he made wine at home for more than a decade before starting his commercial venture. The vintner earned bachelor's and master's degrees, as well as a doctorate, from nearby University of California, Davis.

Not only is the three-story building suitable for production and aging, it's an aesthetically pleasing site for a winery. Visitors are welcomed at a vintage, high-ceilinged room that has been attractively refitted for tastings and retail sales. Storm has furnished this public room with antique furniture and winemaking equipment. The street-level rooms also contain a laboratory and areas for fermentation and case storage. Aging takes place in the cellar.

The Winters Winery roster includes several varietals and two generics bottled as Putah Creek Red and Gold.

15 Main Street
Winters, CA 95694
(916) 795-3201

HOURS: 10 A.M.–5 P.M. daily
TASTINGS: Yes
TOURS: By appointment
PICNIC AREA: No
RETAIL SALES: Yes
DIRECTIONS: Downtown Winters, .5 mile from Highway 128.
VINTNER'S CHOICE: Zinfandel

1986
Sauvignon Blanc
Napa County

WINTERS WINERY

Thompson Vineyard, Napa County, California

ALCOHOL 13.3% BY VOLUME
PRODUCED AND BOTTLED BY WINTERS WINERY
WINTERS, CALIFORNIA   B.W. 4983   CONTAINS SULFITES

SOUTHERN CALIFORNIA

The Temecula Valley Blossoms

Back roads in Southern California? Don't scoff. While they may be less common than in the less populous northern part of the state, they do exist. And although wineries are synonymous with Northern California, there are winemaking operations south of the Central Valley. In fact, Father Junipero Serra planted grapevines at Mission San Diego way back in the 1760s. And before its closure in 1988, little Thomas Vineyards in Cucamonga, established in 1839, was California's oldest producing winery.

Soil and climate conditions in many parts of Southern California have been conducive to growing grapes, but like the once-plentiful citrus groves, south-state vineyards have fallen victim to creeping development. Those winemaking stalwarts around the Los Angeles area that have endured urban sprawl are a dwindling few.

However, California winemakers, being the indefatigable group that they are, haven't given up. Forward-thinking vintners in recent years have opened a rural area around Temecula to winemaking. At least a dozen relatively new, enthusiastic winemaking operations now dot the hilly region, about an hour north of San Diego.

Unfortunately, the fact that the Temecula Valley is still a healthy commute from San Diego is no guarantee that affordable vineyard land will continue to be available. The rising cost of land here has already resulted in a few vineyards being uprooted to make way for more housing developments. As one local vintner surveyed his considerable land holdings, he confided to me that while he hopes winemaking will continue to thrive in the valley, the heady prices being tossed around by developers can be tempting. "I love this business," he said. "But you could built a lot of houses here."

Spending the night?

In Temecula, the Loma Vista Bed and Breakfast, a mission-style home-turned-inn with a no-smoking policy. 33350 La Serena Way, Temecula, CA 92390; (714) 676-7047.

Or, the Temecula Creek Inn, 44501 Rainbow Canyon Road, Temecula, CA 92390; (714) 676-5632.

CUCAMONGA TO TEMECULA

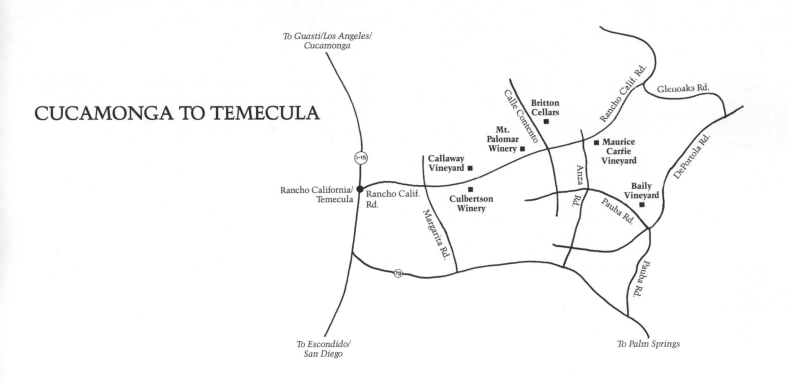

To Guasti/Los Angeles/Cucamonga

I-15

Rancho California/Temecula

Rancho Calif. Rd.

Callaway Vineyard ■

Culbertson Winery ■

Mt. Palomar Winery ■

Calle Contento

Britton Cellars ■

Rancho Calif. Rd.

Glenoaks Rd.

■ Maurice Carrie Vineyard

Anza Rd.

Baily Vineyard ■

DePortola Rd.

Pauba Rd.

Margarita Rd.

79

Pauba Rd.

To Escondido/San Diego

To Palm Springs

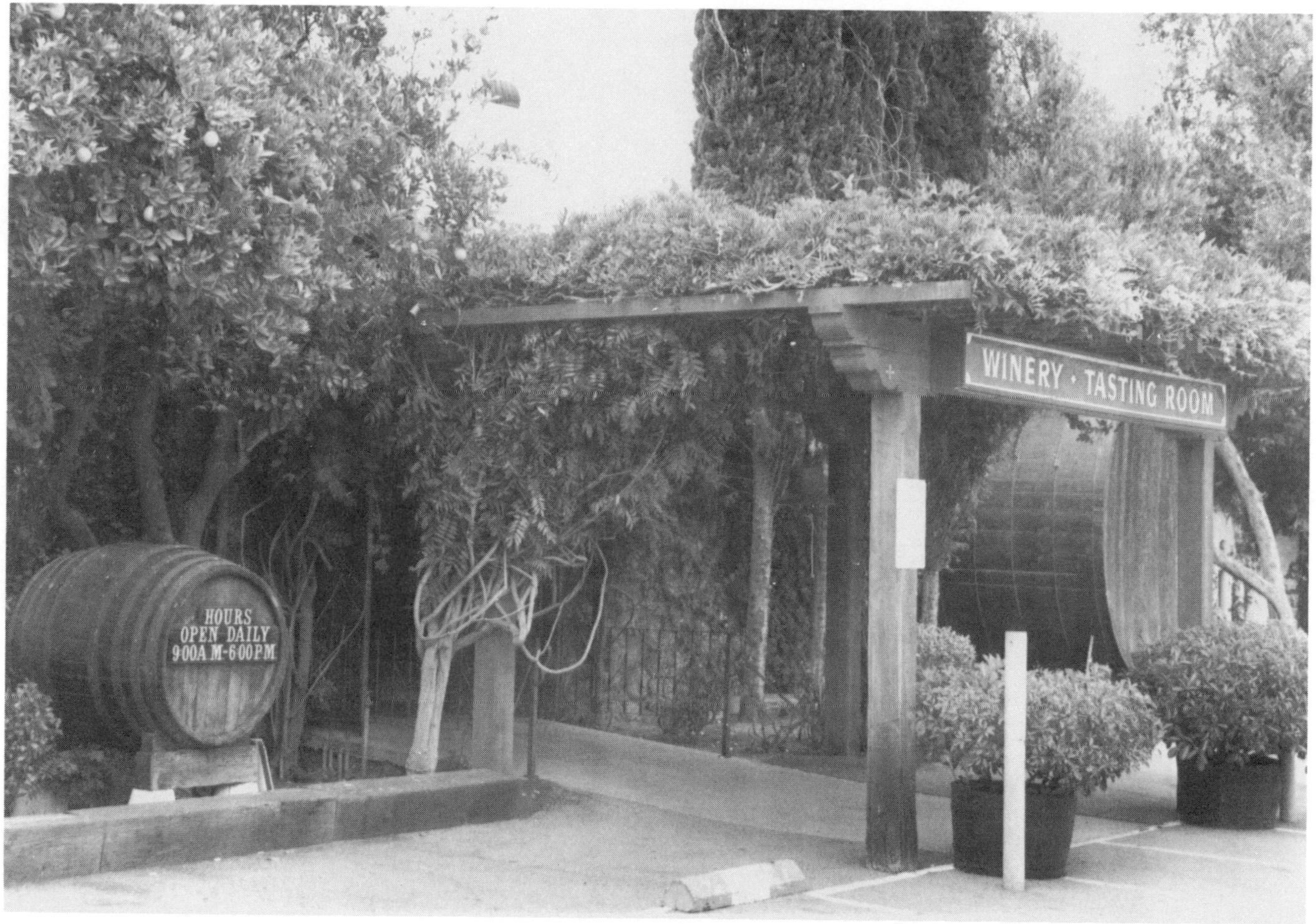
WINERY · TASTING ROOM
HOURS
OPEN DAILY
9:00A.M.-6:00P.M.

Filippi/Thomas Winery
Guasti

I made a long, out-of-the-way trek to Cucamonga to visit what was touted as
California's oldest producing winery. Unfortunately, I was about three weeks
late. The sign on the door of the venerable Thomas Vineyards (Vineyard Avenue
at Foothill Boulevard) announced its recent closure and imminent conversion
from winery to restaurant. I was heartened to discover, however, that at least the
Thomas label is alive and well—a few miles away at Guasti, on the site of
another old winery, formerly known as Brookside.

The family that operates Joseph Filippi Vintage Company in nearby Fontana
owns both the Thomas label and the old Brookside facility, now known as
Filippi/Thomas Winery. No longer a producing winery, Filippi/Thomas operates
as a tasting room and sales outpost for the family's two labels.

Since the winemaking equipment was sold off when the Filippi clan took
over, no tours are available. (All the wines are now made by the Joseph Filippi
Vintage Company.) But visitors won't be bored, considering the number of wines
available for sampling. The weathered old facility is well stocked with just about
every type of wine imaginable. I counted nearly 70 wines—from Grape Brandy
and Mead to Vermouth and Champagne.

2803 Guasti Road
Guasti, CA 91743
(714) 983-2787

HOURS: 9 A.M.–6 P.M. daily
TASTINGS: Yes
TOURS: No
PICNIC AREA: No
RETAIL SALES: Yes
DIRECTIONS: From Interstate 10 northwest
   of Riverside, exit at Archibald Ave-
   nue; south 1 block to Guasti Road,
   left to winery.
AUTHOR'S CHOICE: Zinfandel

Callaway Vineyard and Winery

Temecula

For south state residents interested in an orientation to winemaking and appreciation, Callaway is a fine place to get started. You'll also find this large facility a logical starting point for a Temecula Valley wine tour. Off Interstate 15 on Rancho California Road, Callaway is one of the first in a string of wineries you'll find hard to resist.

Situated on the top of a hill, the vineyards and winery offer a commanding spot from which to survey the valley region. Although its facilities are not necessarily unique, Callaway does approach wine appreciation differently than most wineries. Instead of turning visitors loose in the tasting room, the Callaway folks do some hand holding. Seated at tables, visitors are guided, lecture-style, through the tasting process by well-informed staff who discuss the relationship between certain wines and food. Several wines are offered for tasting (for a small fee).

An exclusive producer of white wines, Callaway was developed by Ely Callaway, a former executive with Burlington Industries. Hiram Walker of Canada bought the winery in 1983.

Each year, Callaway produces about 200,000 cases of Chardonnay, Fumé Blanc, Sauvignon Blanc–Dry, Chenin Blanc–Dry, Spring Wine, and White Riesling.

32720 Rancho California Road
Temecula, CA 92390
(714) 676-4001

HOURS: 10 A.M.–4 P.M. daily
TASTINGS: Yes (lecture-style; fee)
TOURS: Yes
PICNIC AREA: Yes
RETAIL SALES: Yes
DIRECTIONS: From Interstate 15, exit at Rancho California Road; east to winery. The Temecula Valley is 60 miles northeast of San Diego and 90 miles southeast of Los Angeles.
VINTNER'S CHOICE: "Calla-Lees" Chardonnay

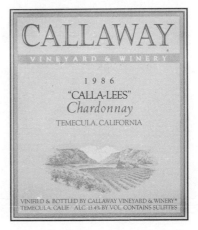

Culbertson Winery

Temecula

John Culbertson's grand winery and restaurant complex is probably the largest expression to date of optimism about the future of the burgeoning wine industry of Temecula. It's obvious John believes folks will be coming out here for some time.

When I visited, the excitement of opening day had barely worn off, and many of the planned sevices had yet to materialize, among them a bottling room and "country inn." However, the parking lot was nearly full, as word had already spread about this impressive new winemaking venture in the valley.

The Mediterranean-style hillside compound is certainly an eye-catcher. There's a waterfall, bright blue awnings, a Spanish fountain, and lots of brass, wood, and trellises.

Upstairs in the winery, John and his wife, Martha, a locally famous cook, have added a private dining room. On the courtyard is a small cafe, which is open without reservations. A "wine bar," where tasting (which includes hors d'oeuvres) is offered for a small fee, and a gift shop occupy part of the winery's first floor.

By no means winemaking neophytes, the Culbertsons drew on several years of experience in establishing the Temecula Valley facility. An oil diving company executive, John cultivated a home winemaking hobby into the first Culbertson Winery, which opened in 1981 in San Diego County.

Not only is the new Culbertson Winery unique in the valley in its physical impressiveness, it's the only area facility specializing in sparkling wines. The Culbertson line consists of a Natural, Brut, Brut Rosé, Blanc De Noir, and Cuvée de Frontignan.

32575 Rancho California Road
Temecula, CA 92390
(714) 699-0099

HOURS: 11 A.M.–6 P.M. daily (tasting room)
TASTINGS: Yes (fee)
TOURS: Every half hour
PICNIC AREA: Yes
RETAIL SALES: Yes
DIRECTIONS: From Interstate 15, exit at Rancho Califiornia Road; east to winery.
VINTNER'S CHOICE: Brut Rosé

Mt. Palomar Winery

Temecula

"There are fortunes to be made in the winery business," a vintner once confided to me. "But it's much easier if you start out with a fortune."

While California's wine country has its share of entrepreneurs who've spun gold from straw, there are probably more who entered the business after achieving financial success in other businesses. John Poole is among the legion of California vintners who traded lucrative business careers for a winery in the country. Although John's first career, as the successful owner of radio stations, didn't offer much of a foundation in the wine business, he sold his Los Angeles–based company and became a self-described "farm boy."

That was more than two decades ago. Today, the Mt. Palomar patriarch is retired, having passed on management responsibilities to son Peter.

The physical winery is fairly run of the mill, but two things impressed me as a visitor. First, there are more picnic tables up here than Gallo has grapes. Even if the Temecula Valley wineries are crawling with visitors, you can be virtually guaranteed a comfortable spot on Mt. Palomar's expansive grounds.

I was also taken with the contemporary label, which, by the way, is much more striking seen in color, with hues of gray and mauve and stripes of silver foil. The new label, I was told, grew out of the refusal by a major wine wholesaler to handle Mt. Palomar wares because of a previous, uninspired label. It seems that these days the quality of a wine just isn't enough to guarantee sales. To consumers sensitive to attractive packaging, Mt. Palomar wines will certainly look tasty. (The product is even better!)

33820 Rancho California Road
Temecula, CA 92390
(714) 676-5047

HOURS: 9 A.M.–5 P.M. daily
TASTINGS: Yes
TOURS: Yes
PICNIC AREA: Yes
RETAIL SALES: Yes
DIRECTIONS: From Interstate 15, exit at Rancho California Road and continue to winery.
VINTNER'S CHOICE: Johannisberg Riesling

Britton Cellars

Temecula

Visitors weren't exactly beating down the doors to Britton Cellars when I made the short drive up the hill from Temecula Valley late one Saturday morning. In fact, the doors were locked. I was almost back in the car before co-owner Tom Freestone casually emerged and invited me in. Britton, personified by Tom, is low key and laid back.

When I asked Tom what the winery hours were, he was hard pressed to nail them down. "We open whenever one of us gets up here (usually around 11 A.M.) and close when we feel like going home (around 4:30 or 5 P.M.).

The Britton Cellars team—Tom and wife, Echo, and Bob and Debbie Britton—carved out the top of a hill above Rancho California Road in 1985, creating one of the region's newest wineries. Surrounded by a California ranch-style covered porch and bedecked with artsy stained glass designed by Tom, the winery is a rustic facility that turns out about 10,000 cases of Britton wine each year (and another 5,000 cases of private label vintages).

The tasting bar is separated from the aging tanks by only a few feet and a wooden railing, which, combined with the proprietors' relaxed personalities, contributes to a comfy, informal tasting experience.

Tom pointed out that some folks have been so impressed with the cedar-walled winery that they've chosen Britton as the site for their weddings. Tom is bemused. "We don't really understand the attraction, but we're happy to help out. We just turn on the lights and let them do their thing."

40620 Calle Contento
Temecula, CA 92390
(714) 676-2938

HOURS: 11 A.M.–4:30 P.M. daily (but flexible)
TASTINGS: Yes
TOURS: Given informally
PICNIC AREA: The winery provides tables on the deck, on request.
RETAIL SALES: Yes
DIRECTIONS: From Interstate 15, exit at Rancho California Road, continuing east; right on Calle Contento (dirt road) to winery at top of hill.
VINTNER'S CHOICE: Zinfandel Pearl

Maurice Carŕie Vineyard and Winery

Temecula

I dare you to drive by Maurice Carŕie Vineyard and Winery without stopping. This is undoubtedly one of the most picturesque wineries in all of California, and it lures wine country travellers like Disneyland draws kids.

Maurice Carŕie is named after Maurice VanRoekel, who, with husband Budd, created the neo-Victorian winery from the ground up. Budd and Maurice, who built the Skate Ranch in Orange County, retired to Temecula Valley and established this facility in 1986.

While the winery, with its 150,000-gallon capacity, is impressive in its own right, the focal point here is the ornate tasting room, deli, and wine-related-gift shop, as well as the expansive grounds, which even boast a classic gazebo. There's also a play area here to keep the kids happy while mom and dad enjoy a taste or two.

The nine or so varieties available at the winery (the vineyards date back to the 1960s) include Buddy's Bubbles (Champagne) and Sara Bella, a Cabernet Blanc named in honor of the VanRoekels' young granddaughter.

Among the items offered for sale here are gourmet picnic baskets (by reservation) that feature quiches, deli sandwiches, chicken, and other tempting creations, along with the wine of your choice.

34225 Rancho California Road
Temecula, CA 92390
(714) 676-1711

HOURS: 10 A.M.–6 P.M. daily
TASTINGS: Yes
TOURS: By appointment
PICNIC AREA: Yes
RETAIL SALES: Yes
DIRECTIONS: From Interstate 15, exit at Rancho California Road; east to winery.
VINTNER'S CHOICE: Sauvignon Blanc

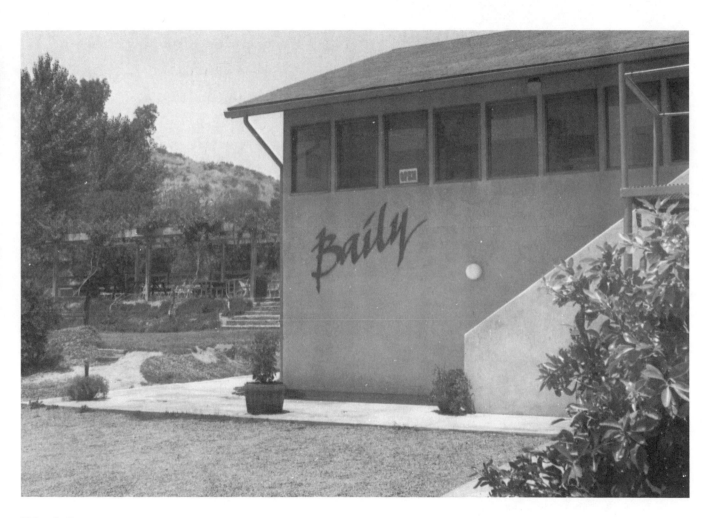

Baily Vineyard and Winery

Temecula

There are two ways to get to Baily Vineyard: the high road and the low road. I took the high road. Wrong choice. As Phil and Carol Baily so aptly put it, "The dirt (high) road over the hills from Rancho California Road is *not* in the book of records as the twentieth century's most harrowing experience. It was at one time, but it's been replaced by backpacking from Beirut to Teheran while carrying an American flag."

If you plan to visit the Bailys' tidy winery (and I heartily encourage it), do yourself (and your shock absorbers) a favor and approach the vineyard from the paved low road (see directions).

One of the Temecula Valley's newest wineries, Baily is typical of California's mom-and-pop-type operations. Phil, who combines winemaking with another career as a computer software developer, works with wife and partner Carol and two strong sons to turn out just over 3,000 cases annually.

Their facility is so compact, the Bailys have had to steer clear of making full-bodied, oak-aged reds, because there's just no room for barrel and case storage. The little winery can be viewed from the railing along the tasting area. What you see is all there is!

When I visited, the family was concentrating on Sauvignon Blanc, White Riesling, Cabernet Blanc, Chardonnay, Cabernet Nouveau, and Muscat Blanc.

In answer to a frequently asked question, the Bailys note, "We don't make Bailey's Irish Cream; we rarely drink it. We have written, however, to tell them they misspelled Baily."

36150 Pauba Road
Temecula, CA 92390
(714) 676-WINE

HOURS: 10 A.M.–5 P.M. weekends
TASTINGS: Yes
TOURS: No (winery can be viewed from tasting room)
PICNIC AREA: Yes
RETAIL SALES: Yes
DIRECTIONS: From Interstate 15, south on Highway 79 for 5 miles, left on Anza Road, right on DePortola for 2 miles, left on Pauba Road .5 mile to winery.
VINTNER'S CHOICE: Cabernet Blanc

Grape Escapes

W hen planning a backroad winery tour, you may wish to schedule your trip to coincide with special wine-related events held regularly in many parts of the north state. Because schedules are subject to change, it is advisable to contact the sponsoring organization several weeks in advance of the dates noted.

Sonoma Valley

Russian River Barrel Tastings, Russian River area wineries, first weekend in March. Call the Healdsburg Chamber of Commerce at (707) 433-6935.

Russian River Wine Fest, Healdsburg, May. Call the Healdsburg Chamber of Commerce at (707) 433-6935.

Sonoma County Harvest Fair, Santa Rosa, September–October. Call the Sonoma County Visitors and Convention Bureau at (707) 545-1420.

Sonoma County Wine Auction, Geyserville, August. Call the Sonoma County Wine Growers group at (707) 527-7701.

Napa Valley

Napa Wine Festival and Crafts Fair, Napa, September. Call the Napa Chamber of Commerce at (707) 226-7455.

Napa Valley Wine Auction, St. Helena, Father's Day weekend. Call the Napa Valley Vintners Association at (707) 963-0148.

Napa Valley Wine Symposium, Napa, February. Call the Napa Chamber of Commerce at (707) 226-7455.

The Central Coast
California Wine Festival, Monterey, fall. Call the Monterey Peninsula Chamber of Commerce/Visitors and Convention Bureau at (408) 649-1770.

Festival of Monterey County Wine and Food, Monterey, summer. Call the Monterey Peninsula Chamber of Commerce/Visitors and Convention Bureau at (408) 649-1770.

Paso Robles Wine Festival, Paso Robles, third Saturday in May. Call the Paso Robles Chamber of Commerce at (805) 238-0506.

The Sierra
Sierra Showcase of Wine, Plymouth, May. Call the Amador County Chamber of Commerce at (209) 223-0350.

The Central Valley
The Lodi Grape Festival, Lodi, September. Call the Lodi Grape Festival at (209) 369-2771.

Wine Tour Maps

Maps that include updated regional listings of wineries along with hours and services are available from the following organizations:

California's Wine Wonderland (complete listing of member wineries). Write to The Wine Institute, 165 Post Street, San Francisco, CA 94108.

Discover the Historic Amador County Wine Country. Amador County Chamber of Commerce, P.O. Box 596, Jackson, CA 95642.

Guide to Napa Valley Wineries. Send $1 to the Napa Chamber of Commerce, P.O. Box 636, Napa, CA 94559.

Guide to Wineries of the Redwood Empire (Napa, Sonoma, Marin, Lake and Mendocino counties). Write to Redwood Empire Association, One Market Plaza, Spear Street Tower #1001, San Francisco, CA 94105 (include 25 cents postage).

Paso Robles Wine Festival Map. Write to Paso Robles Chamber of Commerce, P.O. Box 457, Paso Robles, CA 93447.

The Russian River Wine Road (wineries and inns). Send $1 to the Russian River Wine Road, P.O. Box 127, Geyserville, CA 95441.

Southern Santa Clara Valley Vintners Map. Write to P.O. Box 1062, Gilroy, CA 95021 (include 25 cents postage).

Wineries of Mendocino County. Send 50 cents to the Mendocino County Chamber of Commerce, P.O. Box 244, Ukiah, CA 95482.

Wineries of Monterey County. Write to Monterey Peninsula Chamber of Commerce, P.O. Box 1770, Monterey, CA 93940.

Wine Trails of the Santa Cruz Mountains. Write to Santa Cruz Mountain Vintners Association, P.O. Box 2856, Saratoga, CA 95070.

Primo Picnics

W hen setting out on a backroad winery tour, don't forget to pack a lunch. California's country wineries offer some of the most scenic and least crowded picnic areas in the entire state.

In traveling literally thousands of miles of wine country byways, I've tested more than a few picnic tables (and lingered over my share of Chardonnay). Following are some choices—by region—of the best backroad picnic spots. You'll find addresses and directions under each winery's listing elsewhere in this book.

Before you go, a word of advice. Since most of these areas are maintained "for winery customers," you should drop by the tasting room and purchase a bottle of your favorite vintage before sitting down for your midday feast. (Many wineries even sell chilled bottles.) And be sure to assign a designated driver.

The Sonoma and Mendocino County Region

BUENA VISTA WINERY, SONOMA
The Buena Vista complex, off limits to vehicular traffic, is well stocked with shaded (and sunny) picnic tables.

MILL CREEK VINEYARDS, HEALDSBURG
Picnickers who follow the dirt path up the hill behind the winery will be rewarded with a custom-made picnic deck overlooking the valley and vineyards. You may never want to leave.

OLSON VINEYARDS, REDWOOD VALLEY
Behind this nondescript winery is a lush lawn area that affords nice views of nearby Lake Mendocino.

The Napa Valley Region

Two choices here: one in the valley and another overlooking the valley.

CHATEAU MONTELENA, CALISTOGA
You'll need permission to use the chateau's expansive Oriental gardens, which include a lake, bridges, tea houses, and an old Chinese junk.

VOSE VINEYARDS, NAPA
You can see forever from the picnic deck at Vose. Tables are perched at the edge of those Vose vineyards. In the distance are forests and mountains.

The Central Coast

RIDGE, CUPERTINO
On a clear day, you'll be amazed at how far you can see from this top-of-the-world winery. To the north are the skyscrapers of San Francisco. Below, Silicon Valley sprawls in all directions.

KIRIGIN CELLARS, GILROY
Picnic under the mature trees at this estate, once owned by a millionaire cattle baron.

The Mother Lode and Central Valley

MONTEVIÑA WINES, PLYMOUTH
We purchased a chilled bottle of Sauvignon Blanc at the tasting room and retreated to the shaded picnic tables for a festive afternoon in the golden hills.

BOEGER WINERY, PLACERVILLE
If you're headed in the direction of Apple Hill, I suggest spreading your blanket over a table at Boeger; grassy picnic areas are complete with babbling brook.

R&J COOK, CLARKSBURG
This spot is unmatched anywhere in the state. The Cooks have arranged picnic tables on a quiet levee overlooking the wide Sacramento River.

Southern California

MT. PALOMAR WINERY, TEMECULA
Mt. Palomar's grounds are liberally sprinkled with nice picnic facilities, some of which overlook the valley and vineyards.

About the Author

*B*ill Gleeson is a fourth-generation Californian who grew up traveling the back roads of the Central Valley and the gold country. Gleeson's lifelong interest in the state's byways and hamlets led to the publication of Small Hotels of California *by Chronicle Books in 1984. He is also the author of Chroni-cle's* The Great Family Getaway Guide, *published in 1988.*

A graduate of California State University, Chico, Gleeson resides with his family in the Central Valley, where he works in public relations and marketing.

PHOTO CREDITS
All photographs not listed below are by the author.
The following photographs used with permission:
Haywood Winery: page 18
Adler Fels: page 24
Hidden Cellars: page 60
Navarro Vineyards: page 64
Husch Vineyards: page 66
Schramsberg Vineyards Co.: page 96
Guenoc Winery: page 100
Pacheco Ranch Winery: page 116
Monteviña Wines: page 166
Sierra Vista Winery: page 168

Index